MAKERBOT IN THE CLASSROOM

An Introduction to 3D Printing and Design

Copyright © 2015 by MakerBot®

www.makerbot.com

All rights reserved. No part of this publication may be reproduced, distributed, or transmitted in any form or by any means, including photocopying, recording, or other electronic or mechanical methods, without the prior written permission of the publisher, except in the case of brief quotations embodied in critical reviews and certain other noncommercial uses permitted by copyright law.

The information in this document concerning non-MakerBot products or services was obtained from the suppliers of those products or services or from their published announcements. Specific questions on the capabilities of non-MakerBot products and services should be addressed to the suppliers of those products and services.

ISBN: 978-1-4951-6175-9

Printed in the United States of America

First Edition

10 9 8 7 6 5 4 3 2 1

MAKERBOT IN THE CLASSROOM

An Introduction to 3D Printing and Design

Compiled by MakerBot Education

MakerBot Publishing · Brooklyn, NY

TABLE OF CONTENTS

06 INTRODUCTION TO 3D PRINTING IN THE CLASSROOM
    08 LESSON 1: INTRODUCTION TO 3D PRINTING
        11   MakerBot Stories: Education
        12   MakerBot Stories: Medical
        13   MakerBot Stories: Business
        14   MakerBot Stories: Post-Processing
        15   MakerBot Stories: Design
    16 LESSON 2: USING A 3D PRINTER
    24 LESSON 3: PREPARING FILES FOR PRINTING

35 THREE WAYS TO MAKE
    36 WAYS TO DOWNLOAD
    40 WAYS TO SCAN
    46 WAYS TO DESIGN

51 PROJECTS AND DESIGN SOFTWARE
    52 PROJECT: PRIMITIVE MODELING WITH TINKERCAD
        53   Make Your Own Country
        55   Explore: Modeling with Tinkercad
        59   Investigate: Geography and Climates
        60   Create: Design a Water Tile
        62   Create: Design a Forest Tile
        66   Create: Design a Mountain Tile
        69   Create: Design a Land Tile
        71   Further Activities: Explore Your New World
    74 PROJECT: PARAMETRIC MODELING WITH OPENSCAD
        75   Learn to Code for 3D Printing: Make a Nametag
        77   Investigate: Parametric and Customizable Models
        78   Explore: Modeling with OpenSCAD Code
        83   Create: Customize a Name Tag Using OpenSCAD Code
        88   Create: Write OpenSCAD Code from Scratch to Design a Model
        90   Further Activities: OpenSCAD and Thingiverse Customizer

92 PROJECT: DIGITAL SCULPTING WITH SCULPTRIS
- 93 Making 3D Printed Fossils
- 95 Investigate: Fossils and the Geological Timescale
- 96 Explore: Designing with Sculptris
- 100 Create: Design a Shell Fossil
- 103 Create: Design a Tooth Fossil
- 106 Create: Design Your Own Fossils
- 108 Further Activities: Plaster Molds, Timescale Fossil Dig

110 PROJECT: SOLID MODELING WITH 123D DESIGN
- 111 Experimental Engineering: Build a Bridge
- 113 Investigate: Bridges and Other Load-Bearing Structures
- 114 Explore: Modeling with 123D Design
- 118 Create: Modeling Strength Test Beams
- 123 Create: Design a Four-Point Connector
- 127 Create: Design a Hexagonal Connector
- 130 Create: Design an Arc Connector
- 133 Create: Design Additional Connectors
- 134 Further Activities: Bridge Testing, Upcycled Structures

136 ADVANCED 3D PRINTING TECHNIQUES AND TROUBLESHOOTING
- 137 Using Autodesk Meshmixer In 3D Printing

142 CONCLUSION AND NEXT STEPS

144 ACKNOWLEDGMENTS

INTRODUCTION TO 3D PRINTING IN THE CLASSROOM

At MakerBot, we believe that 3D printing and modeling offer a rich way to enhance and reinforce science, technology, engineering, art, math, and design skills already being taught in the classroom. Presenting real-world challenges to students engages them with a hands-on approach to problem solving.

Everyone's journey when approaching 3D printers is different. It doesn't matter what your background is; anyone can learn to create with 3D printing through project-based learning and experimentation.

3D printing is a tool that allows people to create new things, limited only by imagination. 3D printing and modeling projects should empower your students to take chances and make mistakes. Though it may sound unconventional, we encourage students to fail early and often, thereby acquiring the problem-solving skills and confidence that will convince them to keep trying until their designs succeed.

Use this book as a starting point to help you integrate 3D printing into your curriculum and teach your students the basics of 3D printing. Before you know it, your class will be creating amazing things that you never thought possible.

Inspiration is all around you. We can't wait to see what you make!

The MakerBot Education Team

LEARNING OBJECTIVES

Our goal is to provide you with:
- A solid foundation to learn and teach 3D printing
- Ideas for bringing 3D printing into your classroom
- Knowledge about different types of 3D modeling software and their strengths
- Foundational projects that make it easy to integrate 3D printing into your curriculum
- Confidence to take projects further and tailor them to your students' needs

Our goal is to help students:
- Increase their planning, critical thinking, reasoning, and creative skills
- Develop strong communication and collaboration skills
- Practice visualization and decision making
- Know how and when to use this technology and how to choose appropriate tools
- Learn the importance of iteration in the design cycle
- Understand how to use a 3D printer

3D PRINTING AS A TOOL

Remember that a 3D printer is another tool in your toolbox, one that's immensely helpful for creating a range of objects, both simple and complex. By learning the ins and outs of this emerging technology, you can find new and interesting uses beyond just the printer itself.

HOW TO USE THIS BOOK

Use this book as a starting point to approach 3D printing. In the following sections, we'll share our knowledge and demonstrate a few projects that can be incorporated into your classroom. However, what you can do with a 3D printer doesn't stop at what we've outlined. 3D printers can be a part of any subject if you understand a few basics and think outside the box.

The first portion of this book focuses on how MakerBot Replicator® 3D Printers work and how to teach the technology of the printers themselves. Each section provides you with background knowledge, learning objectives, terminology, example activities, and discussion materials.

The second portion covers Three Ways to Make, the three major approaches to finding models to 3D print. We will go over downloading from an online community, navigating a 3D scanner and designing models from scratch using a variety of 3D design programs.

The third portion of this book focuses on specific project-based learning examples that are meant to be steppingstones to integrating 3D printing into your classroom. You and your students will investigate the subject matter, explore a variety of 3D modeling tools, then create and print original designs. We encourage you to look at the Further Exploration section of each project for ideas on how to tie the project into the rest of your curriculum.

LESSON 1: INTRODUCTION TO 3D PRINTING

While desktop 3D printing has only been widely accessible to consumers in recent years, the technology has been around commercially since the 1990s. Several types of 3D printers have been developed, but throughout this book we'll focus on the technology that MakerBot Replicator 3D Printers use. Let's dive in and learn the basics.

BACKGROUND: WHAT IS 3D PRINTING?
3D printing is the process of taking a digital model and making it a physical object. When you write a document on your computer, you create a digital version, then press "Print" to create a physical copy. 3D printers work the same way, with one more dimension.

Unlike a traditional subtractive manufacturing process, in which an object is carved out of a piece of material, 3D printing is an additive manufacturing process in which an object is built over time by stacking layers of material directly on top of each other. These layers fuse together to create 3D printed objects.

Discussion: Can you think of any other examples of things that are made by stacking layers? (Building blocks, cakes, stones, etc.)

LEARNING OBJECTIVES
- Understand what 3D printing is and how it works
- Know what kind of technology MakerBot Replicator 3D Printers use and the history of the technology

TERMINOLOGY
- **FDM:** Fused deposition modeling, the 3D printing technology used by MakerBot
- **Slicing:** The act of turning a digital 3D model into thin layers used for 3D printing
- **Filament:** Material used to build your 3D prints
- **Extruder:** The "hot glue gun" of your 3D printer; it uses filament to draw out the layers of your 3D prints
- **Build plate:** Surface on which prints are built

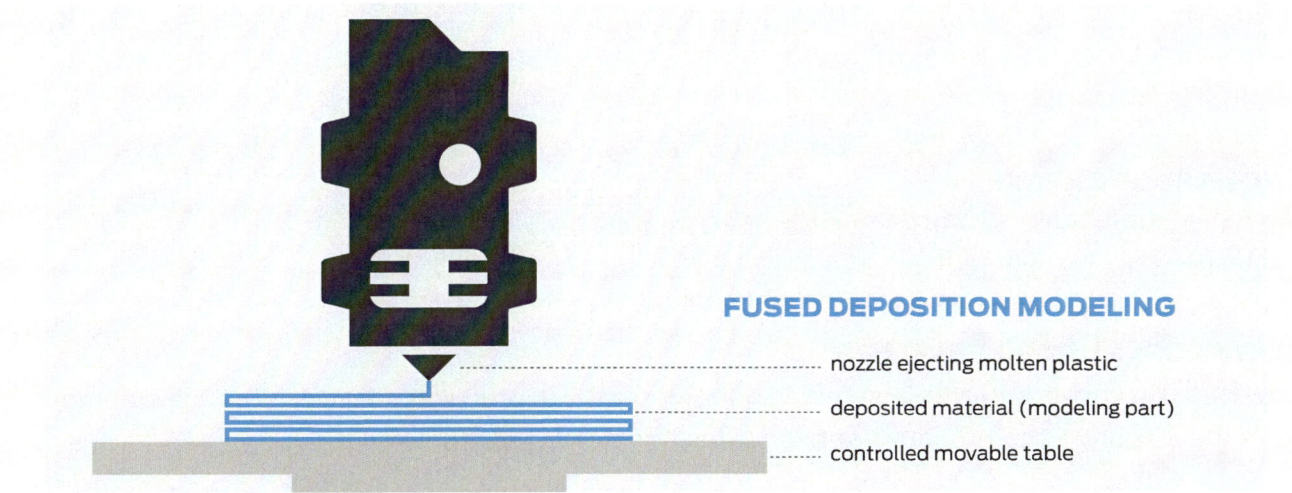

MAKERBOT TECHNOLOGY

Fused deposition modeling (FDM) is the additive manufacturing technology that MakerBot Replicator 3D Printers utilize to create 3D models.

Discussion: What are other 3D printing technologies? (SLA, SLS, PolyJet, etc.)

How does it work? FDM printing starts with a digital 3D model that's "sliced" into thin layers. On the printer, filament is fed into an extruder that draws out each slice, layer by layer. Over time, these thin layers stack on top of each other until your object is finished.

History: Scott Crump invented FDM in the late 1980s by creating a system to draw out layers on an x-y-z matrix. Although 3D printing has been around since then, the technology has only become widely accessible in the past five years. Just like the rise of computers, the 3D printing revolution started with a select few. In 2009, MakerBot brought desktop 3D printers to market and created a new wave of accessible 3D printing.

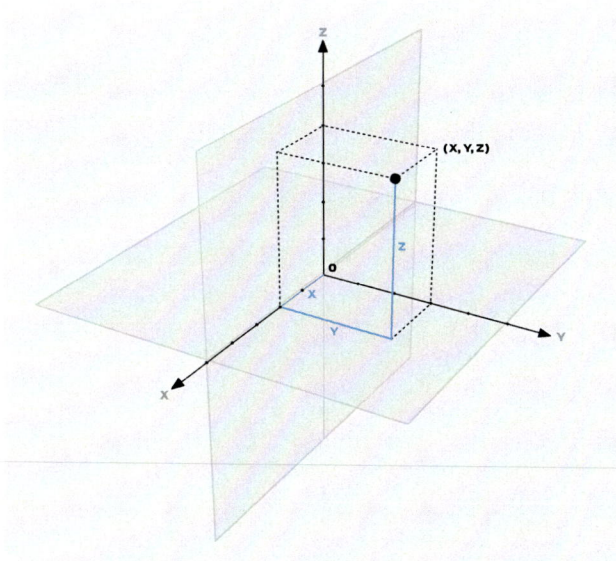

The Cartesian Coordinate System

Activity: Using a hot glue gun, draw out a square. Let it cool and repeat the process, directly on top of the first square. This demonstrates the original idea behind FDM 3D printing. Alternatively, draw out the layers with frosting or whipped cream.

The Cartesian coordinate system is a method for specifying the location of points in a 2D or 3D grid. Every 3D model has its own unique set of coordinates that defines its shape. Our printers use these points as instructions to create your object.

Once a layer is drawn out, the build plate takes a step along the z-axis. Then the next layer is drawn on top. Over time, the layers stack together, kind of like the layers of a multi-tiered birthday cake, to create your 3D object.

KNOWLEDGE CHECKS
- What technology do MakerBot Replicator 3D Printers use?
- How does the technology work?

HOW PEOPLE USE 3D PRINTERS

Now that you have a basic understanding of how your 3D printer works, let's explore the different ways the 3D printing community has been using this exciting technology!

One of the most exciting aspects of 3D printing is the more familiar it becomes, the more your focus becomes what you can make with 3D printers, not how they operate. The 3D printer in your classroom is kind of like an oven: it's easy to operate, and now you and your students can learn how to "cook."

This next section highlights some examples of how people are using their MakerBot Replicator 3D Printers. We hope these stories will help inspire you to think about ways you can "cook" with your 3D printer. As you read each story, be sure to check out the related examples that take a different approach.

Going further: Explore MakerBot Thingiverse® and GrabCAD, great places to get inspiration for your next project. Both are online libraries containing hundreds of thousands of free 3D models to download and 3D print.

MAKERBOT STORIES: EDUCATION

A student's CO2 car with custom 3D printed wheels.

A. MACARTHUR BARR MIDDLE SCHOOL — CO2 DRAG RACE
Topic: Teaching engineering with CO2 drag race cars
Related subjects: Science, math, engineering
Story: Vinny Garrison is the technology teacher and racing commissioner at A. MacArthur Barr Middle School, in Nanuet, NY. Over the course of seven weeks, each eighth grader shapes a foot-long wood block into a car and makes a set of wheels on a MakerBot Replicator 3D Printer. Students eager to challenge the all-time record create wheels weighing less than a gram.

Balloon-Powered Cars
Search Thingiverse for "balloon powered cars." Make balloon-powered cars to explore the idea of energy conservation.

Balloon-Powered Jet Car, by thehans, thing:16987

MAKERBOT STORIES: MEDICAL

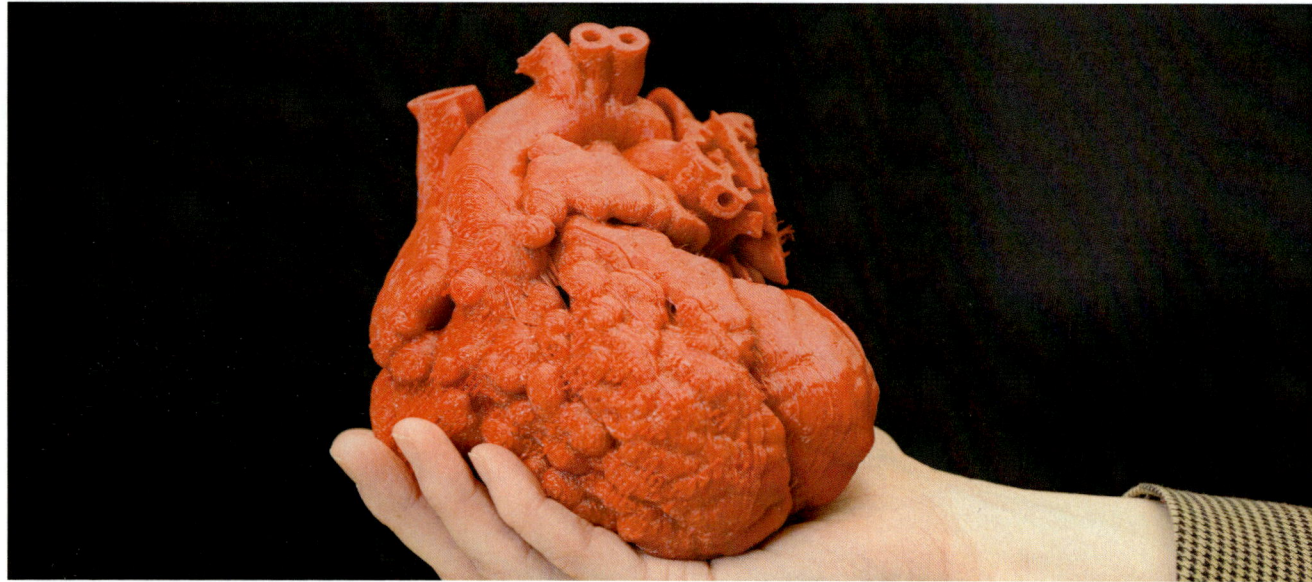

The child's heart was digitally enhanced to be 3D printed three times its natural size.

KOSAIR CHILDREN'S HOSPITAL
Topic: Exploring medical applications of 3D printing
Related subjects: Science, health, medicine, anatomy
Story: Doctors at Kosair Children's Hospital, in Louisville, KY, used a MakerBot Replicator 3D Printer to create a replica of a 14-month-old boy's heart. They converted CT scan data to a 3D printable format to make a scale model. The model was then used to map out and practice the best course of action for performing the procedure, saving valuable time during the actual surgery.

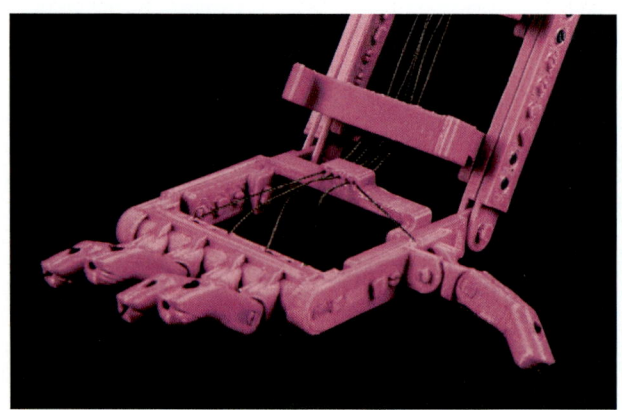

Snap-Together Robohand
Robohand is a low-cost 3D printed prosthetic hand that can be adjusted to fit the size and needs of each user. This open-source project has sparked an amazing community of people offering to print a Robohand for anyone in need.
Snap-Together Robohand, by MakerBot, thing:92937

MAKERBOT STORIES: BUSINESS

All of the electronics that make Kisi function are placed inside this 3D printed shell.

KISI
Topic: Product development
Related subjects: Entrepreneurship, product design, business
Story: Kisi is an electronic lock that recognizes a cell phone app as the key. Kisi employees use a MakerBot Replicator 3D Printer to prototype as well as manufacture the locks. Once a lock is printed, the electronics are assembled into the device. Because the devices are manufactured on demand, each can be customized for the individual client.

Hoover Air Cordless Extended Runtime LithiumLife Battery Mount
Hoover designed a 3D printable snap mount to address feedback from customers wanting a spare battery on their wireless vacuum. They released this file as a free download from Thingiverse.

Hoover Air Cordless Extended Runtime LithiumLife Battery Mount, by Hoover, thing:605278

MAKERBOT STORIES: POST-PROCESSING

This cement lamp is made using a 3D printed mold. Photo © Shane Blomberg.

FOUNDRY CONCRETE LAMP

Topic: Post-processing

Related subjects: Mold making, art, other mediums

Story: Shane Blomberg was inspired to create a lamp that aesthetically mimicked the appearance of hot metal in a furnace. Using a 3D printed mold, he created the shape of the lamp with quick-set concrete. Once the concrete set, he used a heat gun to melt the plastic away. This is a great way to combine both additive and subtractive technology into your creation process.

Lollipop Casting

If you create a food grade silicone mold from your 3D print, you can make any number of customizable eats.

Design Lollipop with 3D Printed Object, by mrtial, thing:661482

MAKERBOT STORIES: DESIGN

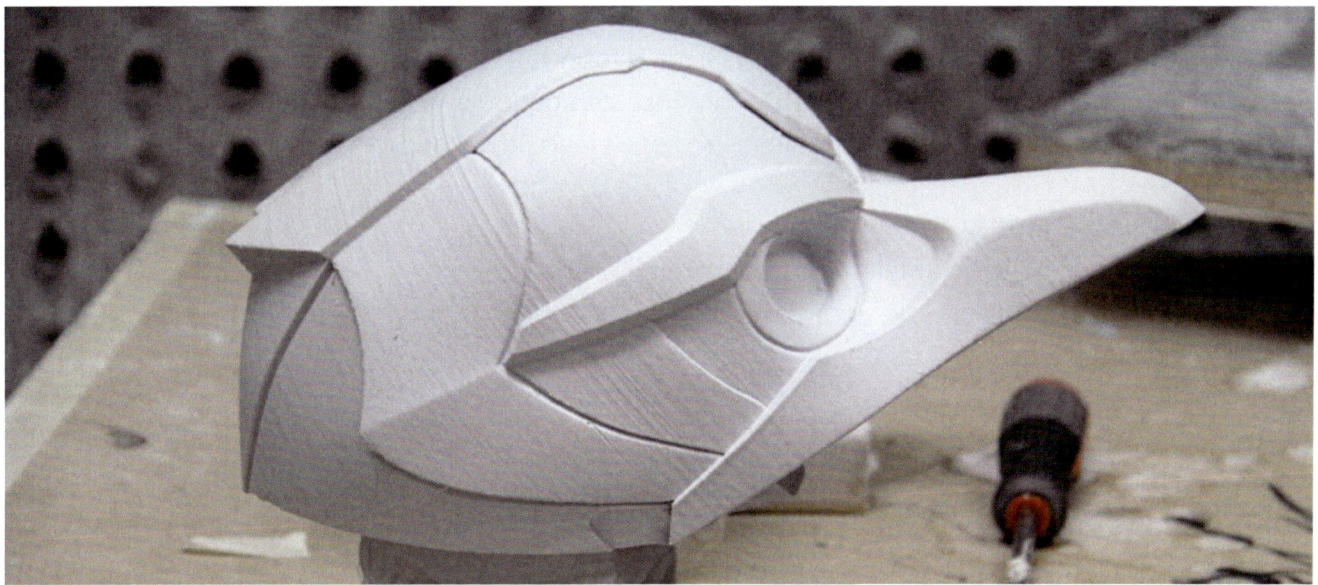

What used to be made completely by hand is now 3D modeled on computers and then 3D printed.

LEGACY EFFECTS
Topic: 3D printing and design
Related subjects: Media arts, entertainment, animation, computer graphics
Story: Legacy Effects is a special effects studio specializing in creature design, prosthetic make-up, animatronics and specialty suits for Hollywood blockbuster movies. Lead systems engineer Jason Lopes uses his MakerBot Replicator 3D Printer to churn out quick, inexpensive prototypes before committing to the production-ready models that power computer graphics-animated movie magic.

Create Your Own Creatures
Create and customize fantastic 3D sculptures and characters like a pro with Autodesk 123D Sculpt+ or Autodesk Tinkerplay, both free design apps.

LESSON 2: USING A 3D PRINTER

Now that we've explored a bit how others are using their 3D printers, it's time for you to get started. Use this book as well as your User Manual as a solid foundation to begin. This book focuses on the MakerBot Replicator Desktop 3D Printer but includes callouts for other MakerBot 3D printers. All material covered should be applicable regardless of which 3D printer you're using.

LEARNING OBJECTIVES
- Understand how to set up a MakerBot Replicator 3D Printer
- Be able to identify and define key components of your printer
- Define leveling and its importance

TERMINOLOGY
- **Gantry:** A pulley and belt system that moves the carriage
- **Carriage:** The part of the printer that carries the extruder on the x-axis and y-axis
- **Build plate:** Surface on which prints are built
- **Filament:** Material used to build your 3D prints
- **MakerBot Replicator Smart Extruder:** The "hot glue gun" of your 3D printer; it uses filament to draw out the layers of your 3D prints
- **Leveling:** Process to ensure proper distance between the nozzle of the Smart Extruder and the build plate
- **Purge line:** Straight line drawn across the front of the build plate at the start of every print
- **Firmware:** The code installed on the printer's hardware that allows it to operate
- **MakerBot Desktop:** Free 3D printing software for discovering, managing, preparing and sharing your 3D prints

UNBOXING AND SETUP
Refer to your User Manual for detailed unboxing and setup instructions. Make sure you're running the most current version of MakerBot Desktop and Firmware before starting to print. More information can be found on page 53 in the MakerBot Replicator User Manual.

The following diagrams detail the main components of each of the printers.

Activity: Study the following diagrams and terminology of each of the printers. After your review, correctly identify and define the main components.

MAKERBOT REPLICATOR DESKTOP 3D PRINTER

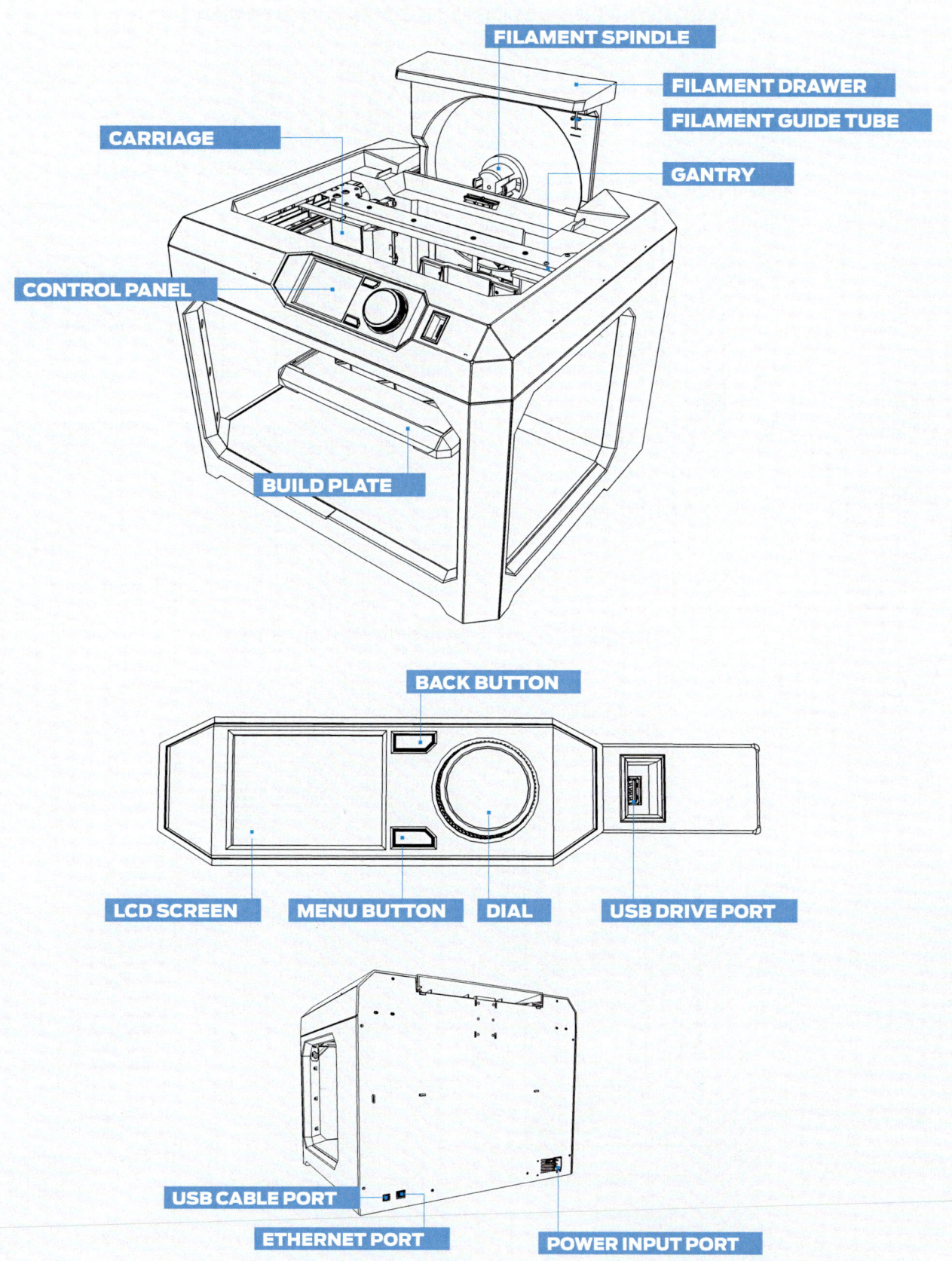

MAKERBOT REPLICATOR MINI COMPACT 3D PRINTER

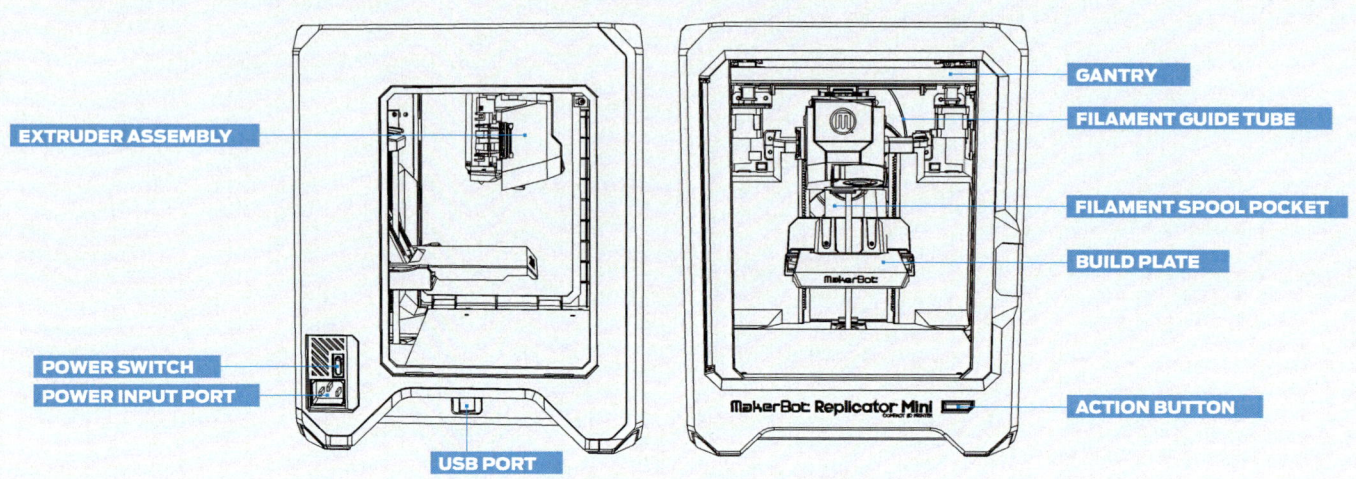

MAKERBOT REPLICATOR Z18 3D PRINTER

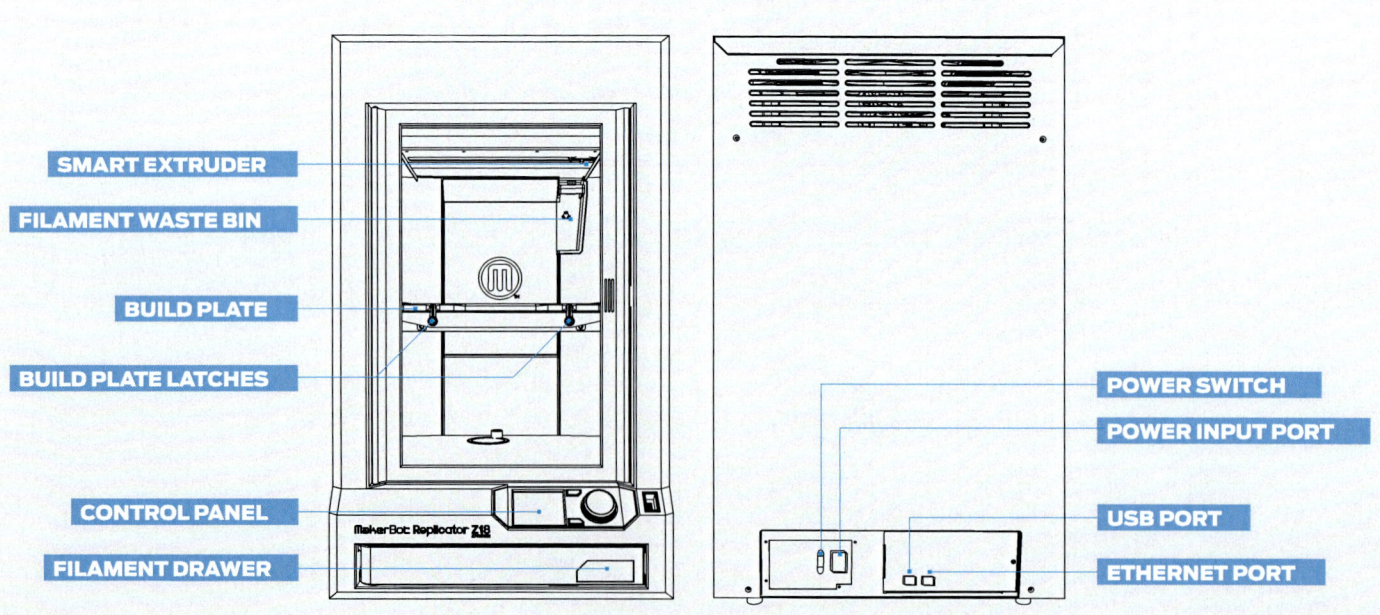

PRINTER SETUP LOGISTICS
Printer and Filament Placement
Placement of your printer(s) can have an impact on its use as well as its performance:
- Set up your printer in a stable location that doesn't have excessive temperature fluctuations throughout the day (e.g., do not place it near an air-conditioning vent).
- It's helpful to have a space near the printer to clean prints off. You'll also need a place for print tools (see Suggested Tools below).
- Store filament in a cool, dry location, preferably in the original packaging, to help guard against humidity.

Other Considerations
- Placing 3D printer(s) in your classroom allows for a lot of student interaction, hands-on time, and printing during class, but lessens visibility and accessibility to the school community.
- Placing 3D printers(s) in a communal space (library, front office, etc.) ensures visibility and encourages use by students, faculty, and staff, but complicates the logistics of printing during class.
- If the printer is in an openly accessible area, keep the filament and Smart Extruder in your desk or in a closet to prevent unwanted use.

Suggested Tools
The following tools are great to have near your printer for print cleanup and post-processing:
- **Thin metal craft spatula** – for removing prints from the build plate without tearing the tape.
- **Needle-nose pliers** – for removing support material.
- **Small wire-cutting pliers** – for removing support material and cleaning off excess filament.
- **Tweezers** – for removing support material.
- **Hand applicator** – for applying build plate tape and smoothing out air bubbles.
  Thingiverse (see page 36) has a large collection of printable tool holders. The task of organizing your tools is also a great opportunity for students to design and print their own tool holders.

PARTS INCLUDED IN ACCESSORY KIT

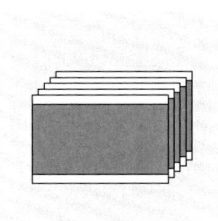

Build Plate Tape
Five precut sheets to apply to your build plate. If you have a MakerBot Replicator Z18 3D Printer, you have one sheet.

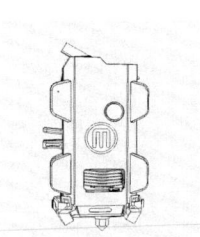

Smart Extruder
The MakerBot Replicator Smart Extruder is an extruder with a lot of built-in sensors. The sensors help detect filament absence and clogs. The extruder attaches to the carriage via magnets and pins.

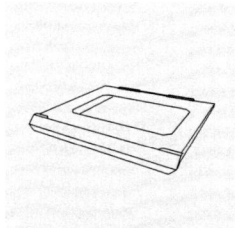

Build Plate
The build plates of MakerBot Replicator 3D Printers vary in type and size, depending on the model. We don't recommend printing directly onto the build plate without protective tape.

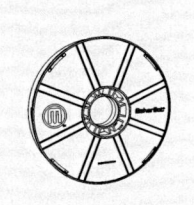

Filament Spool
2 lb spool of MakerBot PLA Filament. PLA is polylactic acid. MakerBot PLA Filament is a nontoxic resin made of sugar derived from field corn and has a semisweet smell (like waffles) when heated.

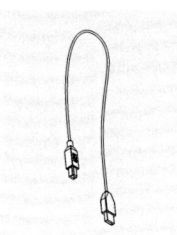

USB Cable
The USB cable is available for local printing or to set up Wi-Fi capabilities.

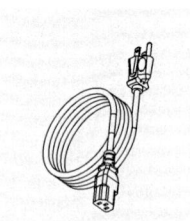

Power Cable
Your printer needs to be plugged into a power source of 100–240 VAC.

Remove Shipping Material
For shipping, there are plastic inserts placed below the build plate as well as a foam brace on the gantry. Remove these three components before turning your printer on. Make sure you keep these materials, especially if you plan to travel with your printer.

FIRST SETUP
Printer Walkthrough

Once your printer is on, there will be a startup script. The walkthrough will prepare the printer for your first print. **Print Menu > Internal Storage** has all the demo prints in case you need to find them again.

CONNECTING TO YOUR 3D PRINTER
Once you've completed your first print, MakerBot recommends connecting your printer via USB cable or Ethernet to download the latest firmware. If you want to connect to Wi-Fi, first you'll need to connect via these other methods. Double-check the connection in the **Devices** dropdown in MakerBot Desktop. If you're connected, it should read **[Your Printer Name Here] (USB)**.

Updating Firmware
You should be prompted to download new firmware if your connected printer is out of date. Double-check in **Devices > Update Firmware**.

Connecting via Wi-Fi
To connect via Wi-Fi, connect either via Ethernet or USB cable to your printer. **Devices > Device Preference > Network** will allow you to connect via Wi-Fi.

PREPRINT CHECKLIST
Before every print, check the following:

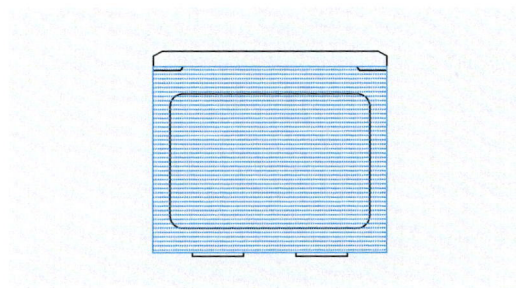

Build Plate Tape Applied
Build plate tape is on the build plate and (mostly) free of tears. If there are more than a few minor tears, remove the build plate and apply new tape before printing.

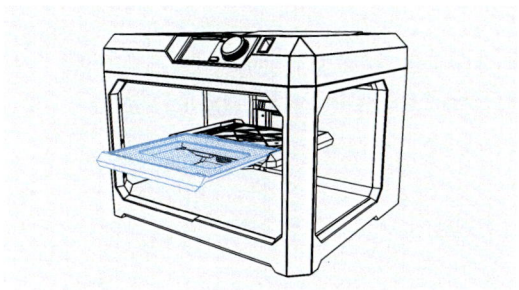

Build Plate Installed
The build plate has been loaded properly onto the Z Stage.

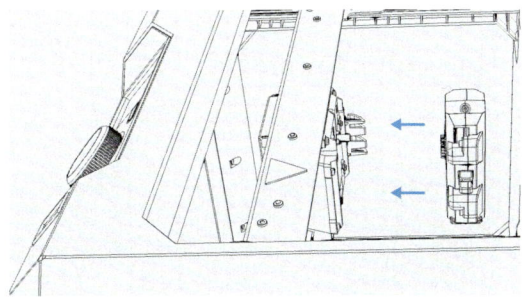

MakerBot Replicator Smart Extruder Attached
A Smart Extruder is attached to the carriage. Double-check that the Smart Extruder is attached by scrolling the dial to **Utilities > Attach Smart Extruder**.

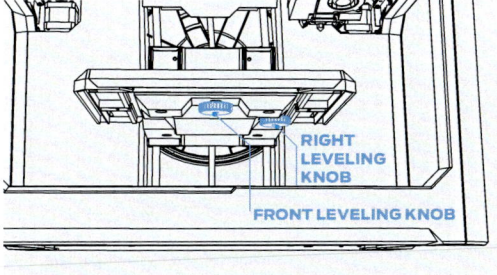

Build Plate Is Level
If you were not the last person to use the printer, you should level your build plate before printing. Scroll the dial to **Utilities > Level Build Plate** and follow the on-screen instructions until assisted leveling is complete.

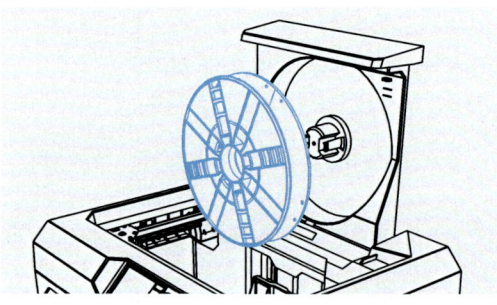

Filament Loaded Properly
Ensure that filament is loaded into the filament drawer correctly. Change filament using the **Filament** menu. When loading new filament, clip off the end, making a pointed tip to prevent clogs in your extruder.

WHAT IS LEVELING? WHY IS IT IMPORTANT?

A level build plate means that the distance between the nozzle of the extruder and the build plate is the same at every point. A build plate that's not level will usually result in a poor print. For example, if the build plate is tilted slightly upward on the right side, then the first layer of the print will be squished on the right side and loose on the left side. The first layer of your print is the most important; it's like a foundation for your house. If it isn't laid correctly, the rest of the house could be affected.

The MakerBot Replicator Smart Extruder tests this distance automatically. All you need to do is adjust the build plate so it's not too close or too far away. If the printer has been moved around recently, or you're not sure when it was last leveled, it's safer to level your build plate before printing. Scroll the dial to **Utilities > Level Build Plate** and follow the on-screen instructions until assisted leveling is complete.

Leveling your build plate is perhaps the most important part of setting up and maintaining a 3D printer. If your prints are not adhering properly, chances are, you need to re-level the build plate.

When To Level
- The first time you unbox a new printer or attach a new Smart Extruder
- After changing the printer's location
- If filament appears squiggly on the first layer of a print
- If you hear a clicking sound on the first layer of a print
- If the nozzle is cutting into the build plate tape or filament is blocked from extruding
- After firmware updates
- When you can't remember the last time the build plate was leveled

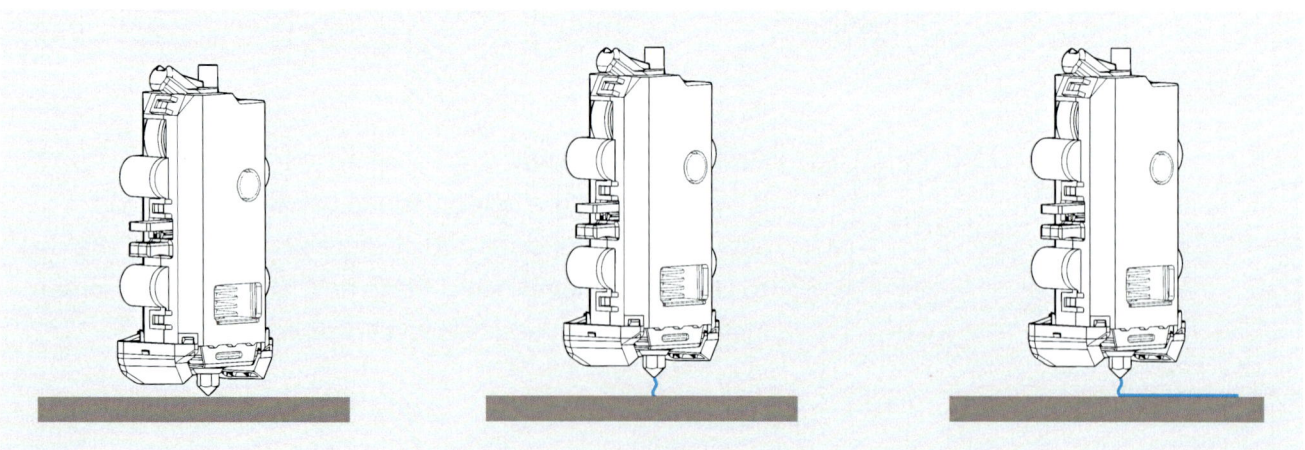

Activity: The MakerBot Replicator draws a straight line across the front of the build plate at the start of every print. This "purge line" can tell you a lot of important information about your printer.

1. Start a sample print. Pay close attention to the purge line.
    a. What does the purge line look like?
    b. What does this purge line tell you?
2. Look at the following purge line examples. Explain what each tells you about the printer.

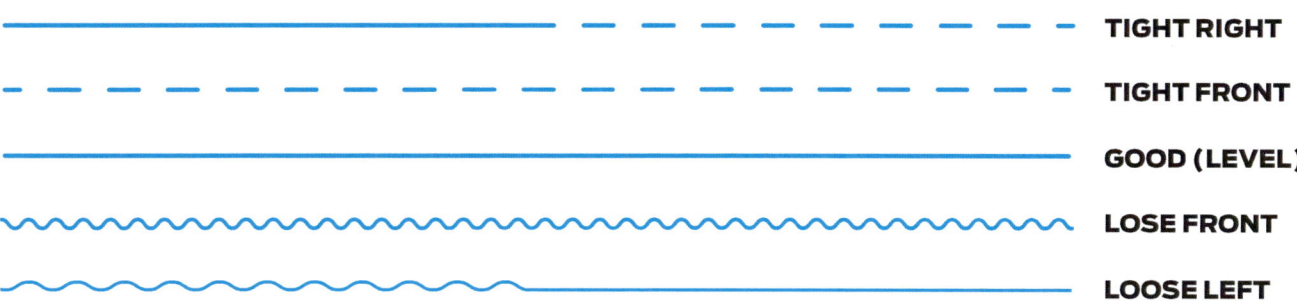

3. Save them! Have students collect, glue, and label them on a sheet of paper for future reference.

KNOWLEDGE CHECKS
- What are the key components of a MakerBot Replicator?
- Why is it important to level your printer's build plate?
- What should you check before starting every print?

I'VE SET UP MY PRINTER; NOW WHAT?

There are two major components of 3D printing with a MakerBot Replicator. One is the hardware, the 3D printer itself. The other is the software, MakerBot Desktop, which prepares your 3D designs for printing. Next, we'll explore how to set up a file for printing and the kinds of settings you can adjust to modify your 3D print.

LESSON 3: PREPARING FILES FOR PRINTING

Once your printer is set up, download, install, and open the MakerBot Desktop software from www.makerbot.com/desktop. The primary function of MakerBot Desktop is to turn 3D models into 3D printable files. MakerBot Desktop consists of five sections: **Explore, Library, Prepare, Store,** and **Learn**. The **Prepare** tab helps you translate from the digital to the physical world.

LEARNING OBJECTIVES
- Explore MakerBot Desktop and its functions
- Learn essential considerations when preparing models for 3D printing
- Use MakerBot Desktop to properly prepare files
- Learn the significance of print settings (resolution, infill, shells)
- Distinguish the main file types associated with MakerBot Desktop

TERMINOLOGY
- **STL:** Stereolithography file format, commonly used in 3D printing
- **OBJ:** Object file format, commonly used for on-screen visualization and 3D printing
- **Build volume:** Maximum physical size you can print on your printer
- **Layout:** Arrangement of STL and/or OBJ files within MakerBot Desktop
- **Thing:** File type for saved MakerBot Desktop layouts
- **Slice:** Process of exporting a .makerbot or .x3g file
- **.makerbot:** File type that MakerBot Replicator 3D Printers use to print; only readable by these printers
- **.x3g**: File type that is used by previous generations including the MakerBot Replicator 2 and MakerBot Replicator 2X
- **Resolution:** The surface quality of a 3D print, dictated by the height of each layer
- **Raft:** Flat surface that provides a large foundation for print adhesion
- **Overhang:** When a layer extends outward, potentially unsupported, over the previous layer
- **Supports:** Removable scaffolding structure built to help parts of an object that are in midair with no material below (see **Overhang**)
- **Bridge:** When a layer prints in the air between two pillars
- **Infill:** Hexagonal support structure built in the interior of the model
- **Shells:** Outside walls that make up the perimeter of your object
- **Print-in-place:** A design with parts that can move immediately after printing
- **MakerBot Cloud Library:** Allows you to access files from the cloud, either on your printer or within MakerBot Desktop

USING MAKERBOT DESKTOP TO PREPARE FILES

On the main screen, there are five options at the top.

- **Explore** gives you access to Thingiverse and the hundreds of thousands of 3D printable objects designed by the Thingiverse community. Use Explore to search Thingiverse for inspiration or new things to print, then save them to your Collections or prepare them for printing.
- **Library** gives you access to your MakerBot Cloud Library and helps you organize your 3D model files. Use it to access things you've collected on Thingiverse or purchased from the MakerBot Digital Store as well as your own original models.
- **Prepare** is where you'll turn 3D models into print files. Bring 3D models into the Prepare screen to manipulate them on a virtual build plate. Then specify print options and send print files to your MakerBot Replicator 3D Printer.
- **Store** lets you buy print files for premium 3D models. The MakerBot Digital Store sells original, fun, and collectible digital content specifically designed for MakerBot Replicator 3D Printers. When you buy a model in the MakerBot Digital Store, a print file for your MakerBot Replicator will be added to your MakerBot Cloud Library.
- **Learn** provides video tutorials on common processes such as Exporting Files, Preparing to Print, and Exploring Thingiverse. Look for new tutorials with each update of MakerBot Desktop. You can also replay the MakerBot Desktop walkthrough in the Learn tab.

To review: Use **Store** and **Explore** to find 3D models, **Library** to keep them organized, and **Prepare** to send them to your MakerBot Replicator for printing. Use **Learn** to view tutorials.

Prepare

Prepare in MakerBot Desktop is where you get to decide how your 3D printer will build your model. Similar to Print Preview in 2D printing, Prepare serves as the utility where you pick your settings. Once you've decided how you want your object to be printed, your 3D model will be translated into a language that the printer can understand. This is referred to as **slicing** a file. The **.makerbot** file determines the path that your printer takes to build your model.

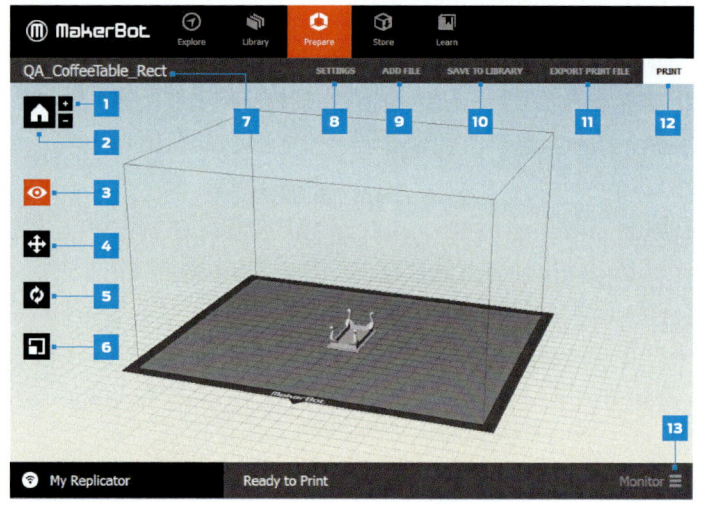

Getting to Know the Interface
In Prepare, various buttons help you set up your layout.

Top Section (7–12)
- These buttons will let you add files, determine print settings, and export files.

Side Section (1–6)
- These buttons will allow you to control the layout of prints on the build plate.

Bottom Section (13)
- This button will let you monitor and control any printer you're connected to.

(Additional information about each button can be found on pages 31–32 of the MakerBot Replicator User Manual.)

Which File Types Can Makerbot Desktop Read?
MakerBot Desktop can open 3D models in the **STL** and **OBJ** formats. These two formats have become an industry standard across nearly all 3D modeling programs. It can also open **Thing** files, which are native to MakerBot Desktop.

Which Files Types Can I Print With?
The printer you select in the Prepare tab dictates which file type your model will be saved as upon Export. Once files are sliced into these formats, they're only readable by the printer.

MakerBot Replicator Desktop 3D Printer, MakerBot Replicator Z18 3D Printer, and MakerBot Replicator Mini Compact 3D Printer: **.makerbot**

MakerBot Replicator 2 Desktop 3D Printer, MakerBot Replicator 2X Experimental 3D Printer, and MakerBot Thing-O-Matic: **.x3g**

How Big Can I Print?
Each printer has a different **build volume**. When you select the proper device in the Device dropdown menu, the build volume will virtually display to show your maximum possible print size.

- MakerBot Replicator Mini: 3.9 L x 3.9 W x 4.9 H in
- MakerBot Replicator: 9.9 L x 7.8 W x 5.9 H in
- MakerBot Replicator Z18: 11.8 L x 12.0 W x 18.0 H in
- MakerBot Replicator 2X: 9.7 L x 6.0 W x 6.1 H in

WALKING THROUGH MAKERBOT DESKTOP

Bringing in a File
Select **Add File** from the top bar in the **Prepare** tab to open your **STL** and **OBJ** files in MakerBot Desktop.

Creating a Layout
A layout is how you arrange your file(s) in your build envelope. You can print one at a time or add multiple objects. You can easily duplicate objects by copying and pasting.

What Do I Need to Consider?
With every file, you need to consider where you want it placed and how you want it oriented on the build plate. You can also adjust the size of your object if needed. Here are some helpful tips for laying out your print:

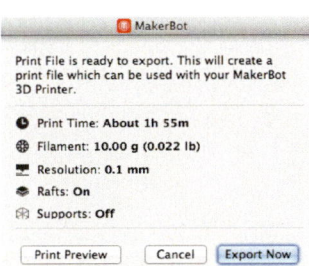

- Place the largest flat surface of your object on the build plate.
- If your object doesn't have a flat surface, pick the section with the most surface area.
- Place print(s) as close to the center of the build plate as possible.
- **Export Print File** and always check **Print Preview** to see how different layouts will build before sending to your printer.

How Do I Adjust the Layout?
Move: Controls the positioning of your object(s) in relation to the build plate. Click it again to open the submenu. **On Platform** and **Center** are useful tools for quickly positioning your object(s).

> TIP: GENERALLY, THE MOST LEVEL AREA OF THE BUILD PLATE IS THE CENTER.

Turn: Rotates your object in relation to the build envelope. Click it again to open the submenu. Use **90° snaps** and **Lay Flat** to flip the object around.

> TIP: CHANGING THE ORIENTATION OF A PRINT CAN AFFECT MANY CHARACTERISTICS OF YOUR MODEL. WE ENCOURAGE YOU TO EXPERIMENT WITH A VARIETY OF ORIENTATIONS TO SEE WHAT EACH CAN AFFECT.

Scale: Adjusts the size of your object. Click it again to open the submenu. **Maximum Size** is a quick way to get the largest print possible based on your maximum build volume.

TIP: IF YOU DESIGN IN INCHES, THE **INCHES » MM** TOOL
WILL QUICKLY SCALE YOUR OBJECT TO THE PROPER SIZE.

Can I Save a Layout?

You sure can! Upload to Library will let you save a layout to the Library tab. You can also **Upload to Library > Save Local File**, which will save your layout as a Thing file.

Activity: Download the file "A MakerBot Desktop Example" (thing: 814499) from Thingiverse. Orient, scale, and copy to match this layout:

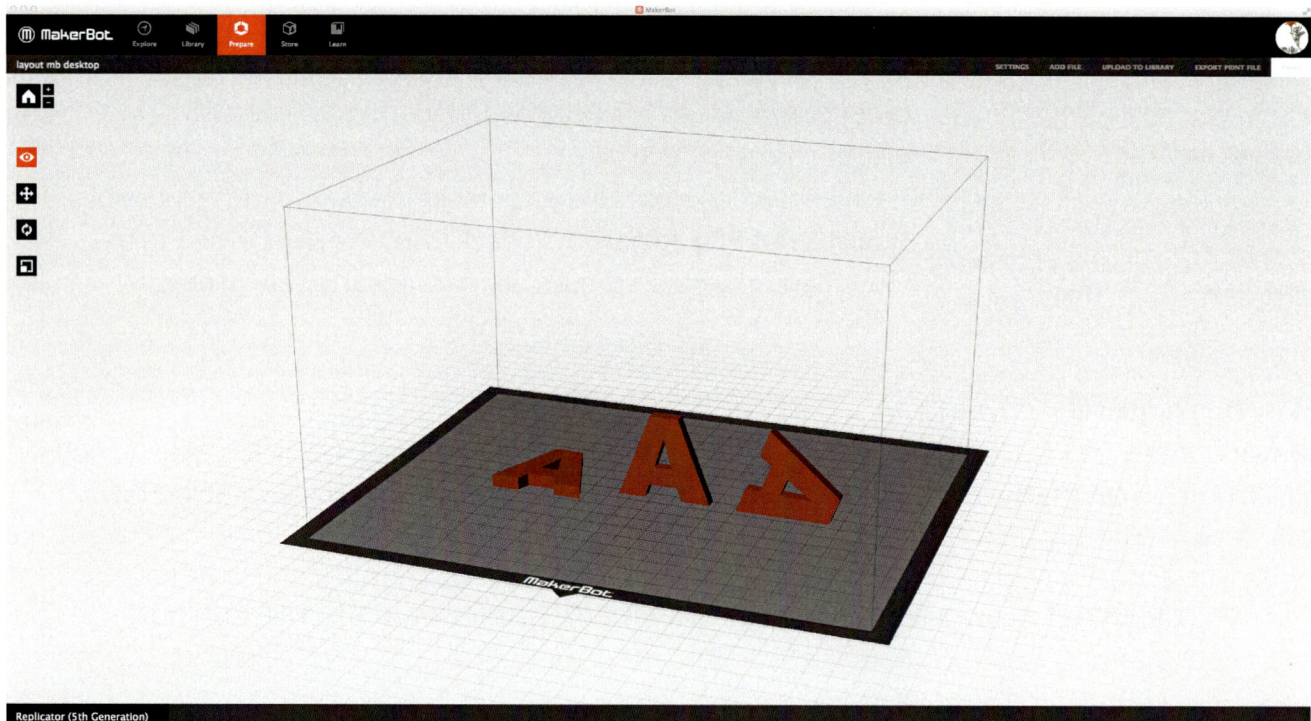

Each one of the letter As can print without support.

What Print Settings Can I Pick?

Print settings allow you to dictate how your print will be made. Print settings will affect the printed object's properties, such as strength, surface quality, weight, and print time. Experiment with some of the settings and note how your prints are different.

Refer to the **Download and Print a Print Kit** section found on page 33 for 3D printed examples of how settings can affect a model's appearance.

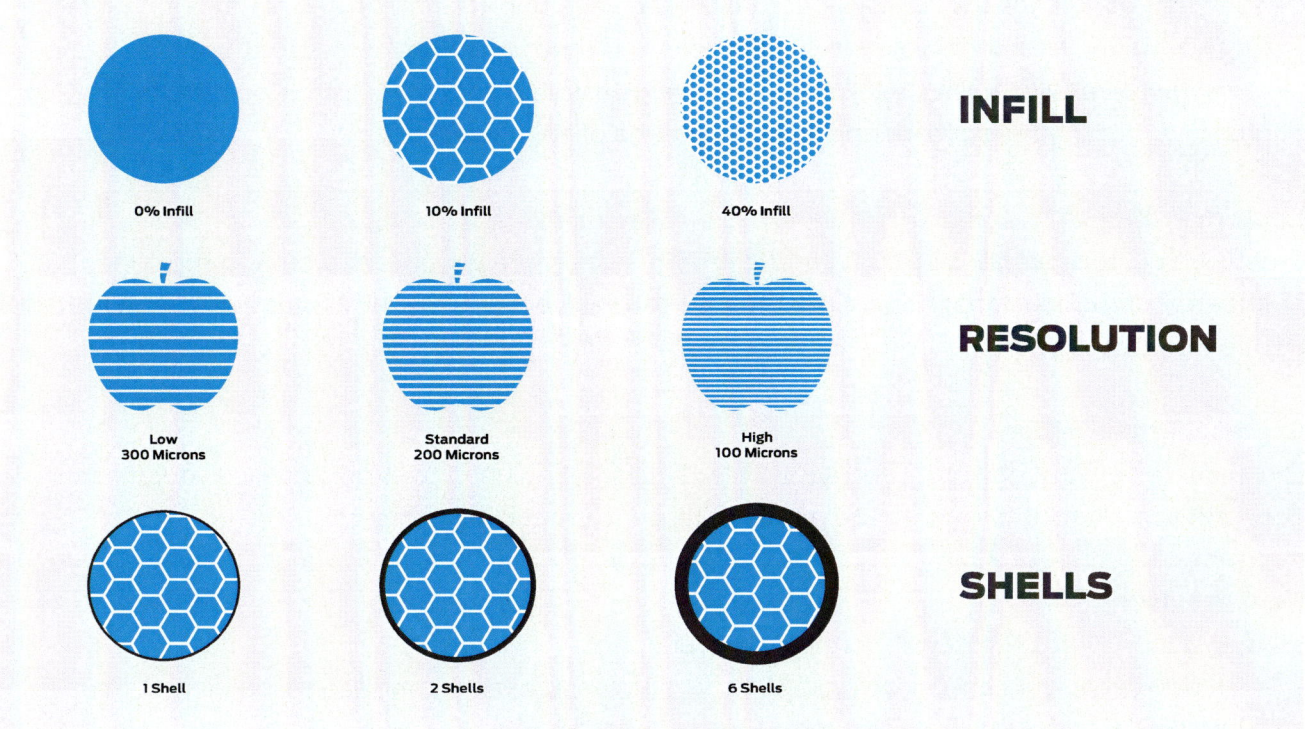

Resolution refers to the thickness of each layer in your print.
- Standard resolution (0.2 mm) is the most commonly used because it's the sweet spot between surface quality and speed.
- Low resolution (0.3 mm) prints draft quality quickly and will have a rougher surface.
- High resolution (0.1 mm) builds very smooth surfaces but will have a longer build time.

Raft: Select the checkbox to have your object built on a raft. The raft acts as a base for your object and any support structures. It ensures that everything adheres well to the build plate. The raft is removable once your print is complete.

Supports: Select the checkbox to have your object printed with support structures. MakerBot Desktop will automatically generate supports for any overhanging sections of your object. Supports are removable using your hands or simple tools once your print is complete. Activate supports when you have an overhang that is greater than 68 degrees for PLA or 45 degrees for ABS. For more information on this subject, check out the Overhangs/Bridges example in the Print Kit section.

Advanced Options
- **Infill** is the internal structure of your object. It can be as sparse or as substantial as you would like it to be. A higher percentage will result in a more solid object, while 0% infill will give you something completely hollow.
- **Shells** are the outlines printed on each layer of your object; they make up the walls of your object. Adding more shells to an object does not affect its external dimension but can increase its strength.

- **Layer Height** sets the thickness of each layer (see Resolution definition above). The smaller the layer height, the finer the resolution of your object. Thinner layers look smoother, but they'll also make your print take much longer. For every layer you would print at 0.3 mm, you have to print three layers at 0.1 mm to make up the same section of your object.

Custom Profile

Creating a custom profile is optional and gives you even more advanced access to the code that prepares your models for printing. Click Create Profile, give it a name, pick a template, and Edit Profile to view the code.

Export & Print Preview

Once you've set your object(s) and saved your settings, you need to export or slice your file to generate a .makerbot file, which the printer will use to create your object.

Print Preview
- Always check **Print Preview** before starting your print
- Scroll down to Layer 1 and move up layer by layer to ensure your foundation is building correctly
- Pay attention to the estimated material use and print time

As a general rule of thumb, if something looks wrong in Print Preview, it's going to cause an issue during printing. Here are some of the most common troubleshooting tips:

PROBLEM	POSSIBLE CAUSE	POSSIBLE SOLUTION
Imported model is extremely small in the MakerBot Desktop view.	Your model may have been made in inches, while Desktop is interpreting the model in millimeters.	Click **Scale** and then select the **Inches » mm** button one time to resize the model.
Model does not adhere well to the build plate while printing.	The build plate of your 3D printer may not be level.	Run through the **Utilities > Level Build Plate** procedure on your printer.
Build plate has been leveled, but model still does not adhere well to the plate while printing.	1. Your model has a small surface area in contact with the build plate. 2. Your model is an organic shape and doesn't have a flat bottom. 3. Your model has a large surface area but is crooked on the build plate.	Use the **Turn** menu to maximize surface contact. Also ensure that **Raft** and **Supports** are checked in the **Settings** menu.
Parts of the model print in the air or have loops of plastic hanging off them.	Your model may have **Overhangs** that require 3D printed **Support** structures.	From the **Settings** tab, make sure that the **Supports** box is checked.

Activity
1. Open your layout from the previous activity, "A MakerBot Desktop Example," and change the model's orientation so it's flat on the build plate. Then slice the file with the following settings:
   - Standard resolution
   - Raft on
   - Supports off
   - 20% infill
   - 3 shells

   Once the file is sliced, record the estimated print time and material use.
2. Change your settings so that the estimated print time is less than 20 minutes. Record the settings that you changed to achieve this.
3. Reset your default settings, and instead of changing your settings to affect print time, change the print's scale. Scale your object smaller so that the estimated print time is less than 15 minutes.

PRINTING LOGISTICS

Printing During Class
- Many objects you make will require 30 or more minutes of print time. Try to plan mid-class prints appropriately based on this.
- Start an example print at the beginning of class to complement what you're teaching that day.
- Start a student file at the beginning of class so that the last 10–15 minutes of class can be used to discuss successes and failures of the object.

Printing Between Classes
- For large projects, you'll have a lot of student files to print. Determine the amount of time you have to print and plate your items appropriately, getting as many prints onto the build plate as you can fit within the timeframe.
- Always check the following before leaving a long print unattended:
  - Print Preview — ensure all files are 3D printable and oriented correctly. If one object fails, then the whole plate will likely fail.
  - First layer — ensure that the first layer prints smoothly before walking away from the printer!

File Management
- Sorting through and plating files can be time consuming. Lots of teachers have figured out ways to deal with this. Read through some of the tips below to get some ideas.

Communal Storage
- Use Google Drive, Dropbox, or even a shared USB stick to keep all student files in one location.
- Have students name their files with their name, a date, and a revision (if applicable).
- Have students upload the STL or OBJ file as well as a pre-sliced .makerbot file if they each have access to MakerBot Desktop.

Find Student Experts
- Chances are, one or more of your students are going to be really interested in 3D printing. This is a great opportunity for them to act as leaders. If you've identified any student experts, have them help manage the print queue. They can also manage the communal storage, slice files for printing, and teach other best practices to their classmates.

Rules
- Implement a print time and/or material limit on prints to save time and materials.

KNOWLEDGE CHECKS
- What is MakerBot Desktop and why do you need to use it?
- How do print settings work and which options can you pick from?
- Which file types can you import and export from MakerBot Desktop?
- What should you consider when preparing a model for 3D printing?

LET'S GET PRINTABLE OBJECTS

Now that we've reviewed how to get a file to your 3D printer using MakerBot Desktop, let's discuss the types of resources available to help you find and design objects. One of the most approachable ways to get started is to join a 3D modeling community and download existing designs, which we will cover in depth within the next section. Go to Thingiverse.com and log in with your MakerBot account for the next lesson.

DOWNLOAD AND PRINT A PRINT KIT

Use this Print Kit as a visual aid while teaching your students about 3D printing. Each print will cover basic concepts, terminology, and/or settings that are found within MakerBot Desktop. The prints included are tangible examples to help further the understanding of this technology. You can find these models on **Thingiverse under the MakerBot Learning account**. We encourage you to print out each of the following to use alongside your 3D printer!

PRINT KITS

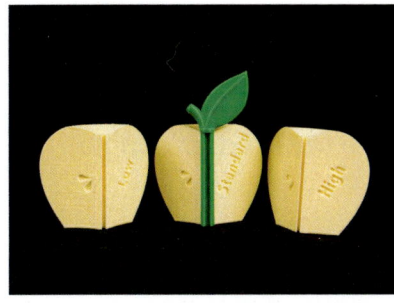

Resolution
- These three prints were prepared at different resolutions: high, standard, and low. Resolution refers to the surface quality of your 3D print, dictated by the height of each layer.
- **Discussion:** The high-resolution print has the thinnest layers but takes longer to print. Why?

Overhangs/Bridges
- An overhang is when a layer extends outward, potentially unsupported, over the previous layer. PLA prints can achieve an angle of 68 degrees from vertical without supports.
- A bridge is when a layer prints in the air between two pillars. PLA prints can achieve a two-inch bridge without needing supports.

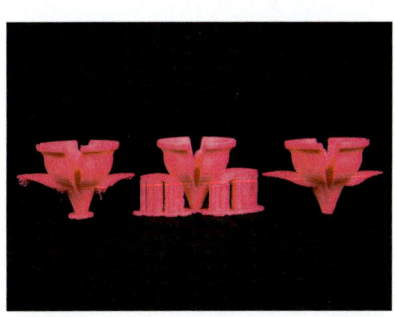

Raft and Supports
- Supports are printed scaffolding for overhangs.
- A raft helps with adhesion to the build plate.
- Remove both the raft and supports after a print finishes.

Infill and Shells
- Infill is the hexagonal pattern that supports the inside of your model. It's represented by percentages beginning with 0%, which is completely hollow.
- Shells are the outside walls that make up the perimeter of your object. Increasing the number will only add to the interior of your object and never affect the exterior dimensions.

Print-in-Place
- Print-in-place files are designs with parts that can move immediately after printing. A lot of thought can go into designing print-in-place files, especially in regard to incorporating **bridges** and **overhangs** creatively in your design. Make sure you don't print these files with **supports**, because the moving parts will be filled in with the extra material.

Assembly

- Assemblies are models broken up into different pieces for printing, then assembled together, to allow you to print in multiple colors or create objects larger than your build plate. You can get creative with how you design your object; breaking it down into multiple pieces can reduce the need for support material.

Explore Thingiverse

Use the community as a resource to add designs to your classroom's Print Kit. As we go further in this book, you'll have the tools to move forward and design your own objects to expand this resource even more. Upload your class's amazing designs to Thingiverse with the tag of "MakerBotEDU" so we can see what you've created.

THREE WAYS TO MAKE

There are three major approaches to finding models to 3D print: download, scan, design. Throughout the next three sections, we'll take a deeper look at each of the Three Ways to Make.

Download
Finding files and downloading them to 3D print is an easy way to get started using your printer. There are many places online where you can either download for free or purchase files. As a source of inspiration, find a designer you like and explore what makes his/her designs print successfully. Try to reverse engineer an interesting design. You can also download files and incorporate them into your own custom designs.

Scan
3D scanning is an exciting technology that offers a quick way to translate real objects into 3D files you can print. Scanning an object enables you to obtain a 3D model without using 3D modeling software. Once you have scanned an object, you can print it directly, change its size, or alter its details. If you have the MakerBot Digitizer, this section will help you optimize your scanning. Keep in mind that this section is completely optional and not a requirement for using a 3D printer.

Design
Learning how to 3D design is invaluable to creating your own 3D printable files. There are many different 3D modeling programs available, both free or at a cost, and depending on what kinds of objects you want to make, you might need to learn a few programs. Make sure you try as many software programs as you can, because each software has its own unique strengths.

WAYS TO DOWNLOAD

LEARNING OBJECTIVES
- Explore Thingiverse and GrabCAD and define their use
- Use Thingiverse to find inspiration and engage with the community
- Understand Creative Commons attribution

WHAT IS DOWNLOAD?
Download is tapping into ever expanding 3D printing communities such as Thingiverse or GrabCAD to access completely free files. Resources like this are an amazing place for inspiration!

TERMINOLOGY
- **Thing:** Free design file uploaded by a Thingiverse community member
- **Likes:** Uncategorized list of favorite designs to show support for their creators
- **Collection:** A curated folder of things you've categorized. Collections can be viewed by other users and are a great way to organize things for students.
- **Makes / I Made One:** When a user downloads and prints another designer's object and uploads a picture. **Makes** help demonstrate that a model can be printed successfully and are also a great way to show support for the designer.
- **Attribution:** Anytime you print and share anything, make sure you remember who made it! Thing Tags can be easily generated at the bottom of each thing's page. Remind students that when displaying these objects in public, it's vital to give credit to the community members who created them. Tagging is a great way to thank them for their amazing contributions!
- **Remix:** Anytime you download a file, alter it in some way, and re-upload it, attributing the original model to the creator
- **Customizer:** An app built into Thingiverse that gives users the ability to customize 3D models with easy-to-use sliders, text fields, and dropdowns. It's based on the programming language OpenSCAD.
- **Groups:** Community-driven collections of things and discussion boards for specific topics

MakerBot Man Cupid by MakerBot is licensed under the **Creative Commons - Attribution** license.

CREATIVE COMMONS
The Creative Commons license allows our open-source community to share objects freely, while providing parameters for how members give attribution and use the objects.

Discussion: Why is it important to give attribution when using someone else's file? How do Creative Commons guidelines help provide a platform for sharing?

WHAT CAN I DO WITH THINGIVERSE?

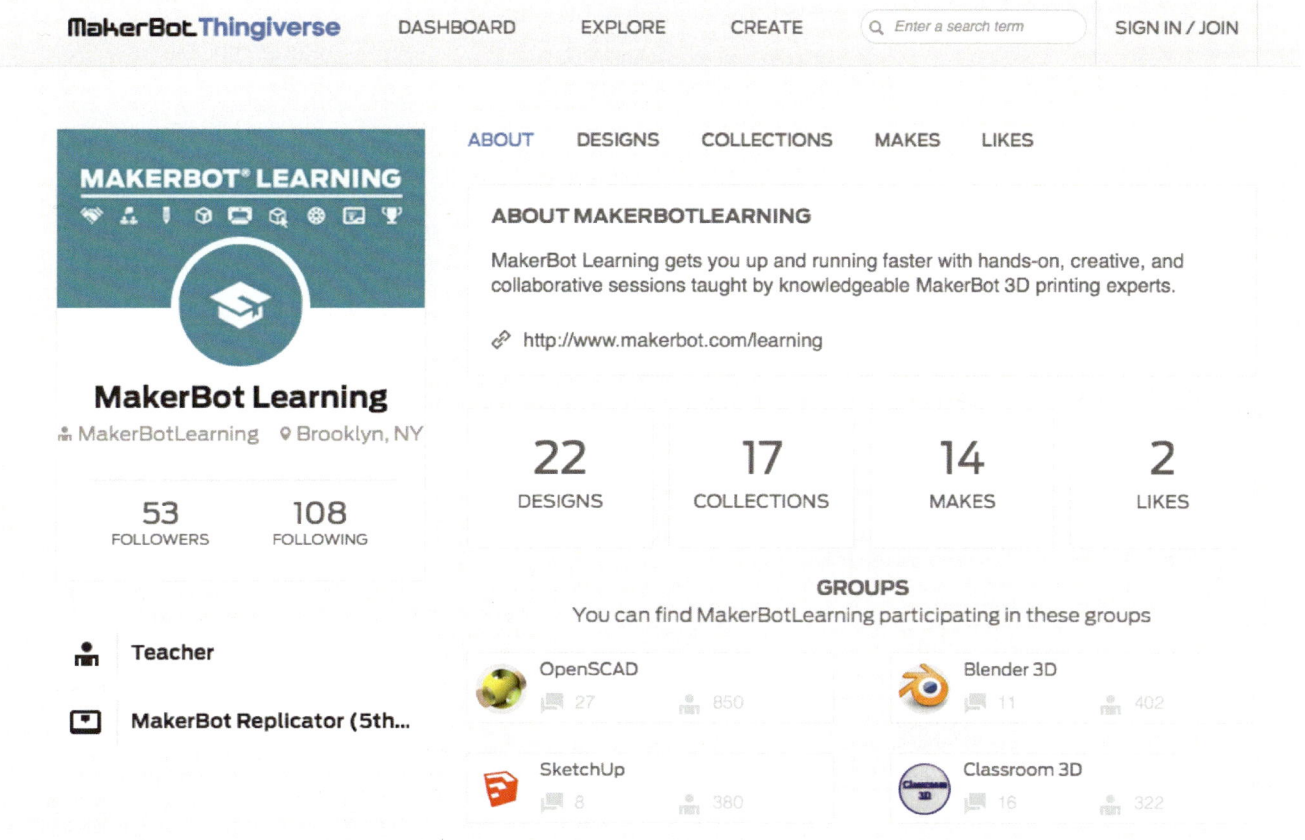

A Thingiverse user page.

Because Thingiverse is built on a principle of sharing, it encourages users to collaborate through community engagement. Whether you post your own thing, download and remix someone else's, or just show support in the comments, Thingiverse is a great way to engage with other people excited about making. Thingiverse groups enable teachers and students across the world to interact and discuss 3D printing.

Here are some activities that highlight a few of the main ways to use Thingiverse. These only scratch the surface; the possibilities are endless!

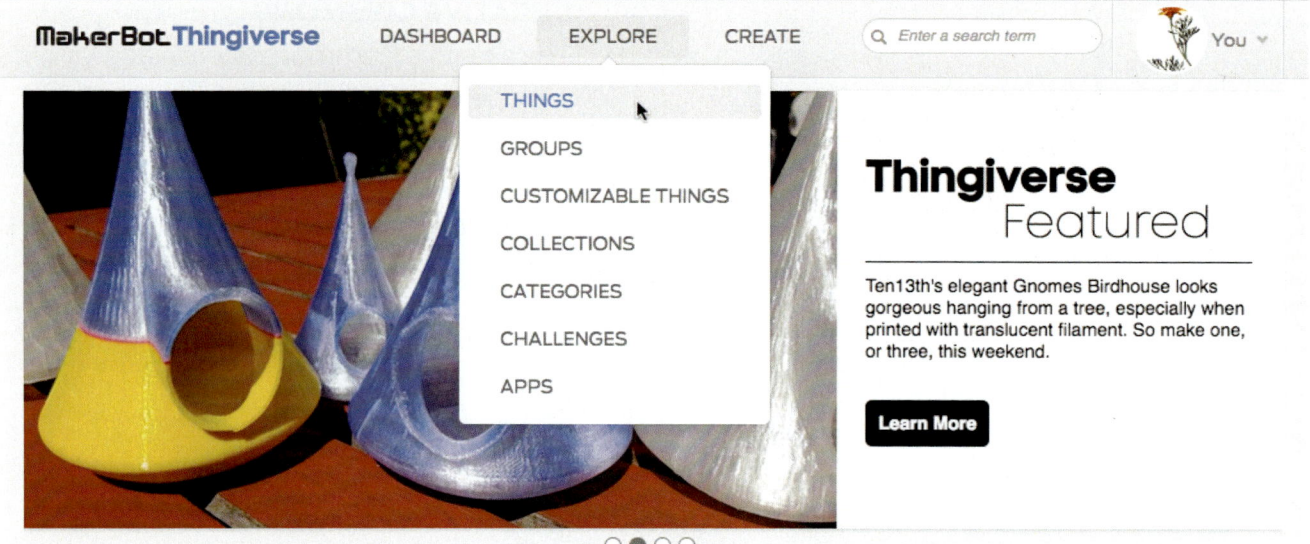

The homepage updates weekly with featured things that can inspire you.

Thingiverse is a great place to start when first exploring 3D printing. Use the **Explore** tab and the search function to start collecting some objects you want to 3D print.

Activity: Spend some time collecting objects that fit the subject matter you're covering. For example, for a history class, you could find five prints that showcase medieval inventions. Check out MakerBot Learning's collections if you need more inspiration.

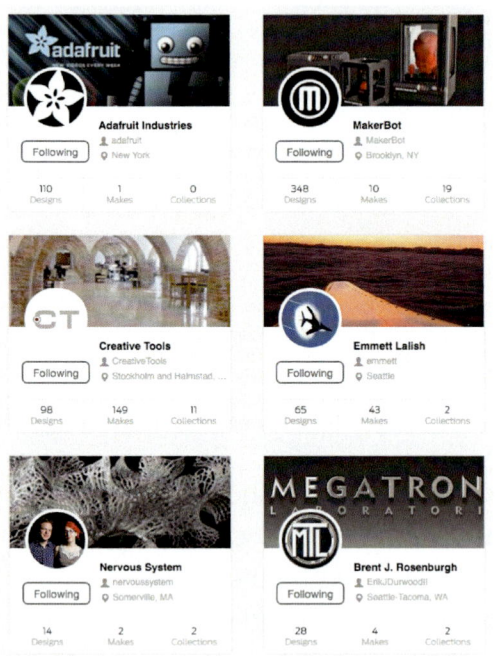

Activity: Find five inspirational users to follow. Explain why you like their work.

Activity: Create a presentation to showcase a user and one of his or her designs. Evaluate the successes and failures of the design. Is there anything to account for when printing? What would you do differently if you were the designer?

- Take it further! Write a fictional story about your designer. For example, werd10 is a ninja by night, but spends his days 3D modeling pencil holders in the shape of his favorite animal, the blowfish.

Activity: Check out Three Heart Gears (thing:243278), by incredible Thingiverse user emmett. Find two or three remixes from this thing and share them with the class. What parts of the design were changed? If you were to remix this design, what would you change?

Further Exploration
Thingiverse is an integral resource for designers, engineers, and enthusiasts alike. Throughout this book, we'll continue to reference and tie in using Thingiverse in a variety of ways to find things, get inspired, and engage with the community.

Activity
Start a class or school-wide Thingiverse account and let each student select a design that they think will improve your classroom or school in some way. Prompt them to write explanations on note cards and post them near the printed objects around the classroom or school.

GRABCAD
GrabCAD offers an online community that offers free downloads of 3D designs specifically tailored for engineers. It's a great place to find a variety of different files ranging from program-specific projects to model renderings to 3D printable objects. It also has a large selection of user-created tutorials on how to make models in specific programs. Like Thingiverse, it's community-driven and a great way to engage with like-minded people exploring 3D printing and modeling.

Discussion: After exploring both Thingiverse and GrabCAD, discuss the similarities and differences with your class.

KNOWLEDGE CHECKS
- What is a Creative Commons license?
- What is a remix and how does it work?
- What are some of the ways to use Thingiverse?
- What are the differences between Thingiverse and GrabCAD?

WAYS TO SCAN

LEARNING OBJECTIVES
- Understand how to use 3D scanning in your classroom
- Know how to set up and scan with the MakerBot Digitizer™ Desktop 3D Scanner
- Be able to identify different attributes that can make your scan successful

WHAT IS 3D SCANNING?
3D scanning is the process of taking an object and creating a digital representation of it. There are a variety of scanning technologies out there. The MakerBot Digitizer works with a laser and camera mechanism. There are many other types of technologies that use a series of cameras and other methods of scanning such as 123D Catch or using a Microsoft Kinect. 3D scanning is by no means mandatory for the 3D printing process, but can be added to expand your toolkit for making.

TERMINOLOGY
- **Point cloud:** In a coordinate system, data points that represent an object's surface
- **Mesh:** A collection of vertices, edges, and faces that defines the shape of a 3D model
- **Watertight:** A continuous outside surface (or **mesh**), necessary for successful 3D printing. For example, an object like a donut, even though it has a hole in the middle, has a continuous outside surface and can be 3D printed.

MAKERBOT DIGITIZER
The MakerBot Digitizer lets you quickly turn the things in your world into 3D models that you can modify, improve, share, and 3D print. The file you get from your scan is a great starting point for something new.

Quick Facts
Biggest scannable dimensions: 8 x 8 in cylinder
Smallest scannable dimensions: 2 x 2 in cylinder
Dimensional accuracy: +/−2 mm

HOW DOES IT WORK?

- **Laser & Camera:** A red laser line is projected onto the surface of an object. As the object rotates, the camera picks up the laser line and processes it into data points, known as a point cloud.
- **Turntable:** The turntable spins the object so the camera can capture all its parts and contours incrementally.
- **Point Cloud:** Data points in space recreate the object's surface digitally.
- **Mesh:** The point cloud is stitched together by the software to create a representation of your object with a complete, watertight mesh surface.

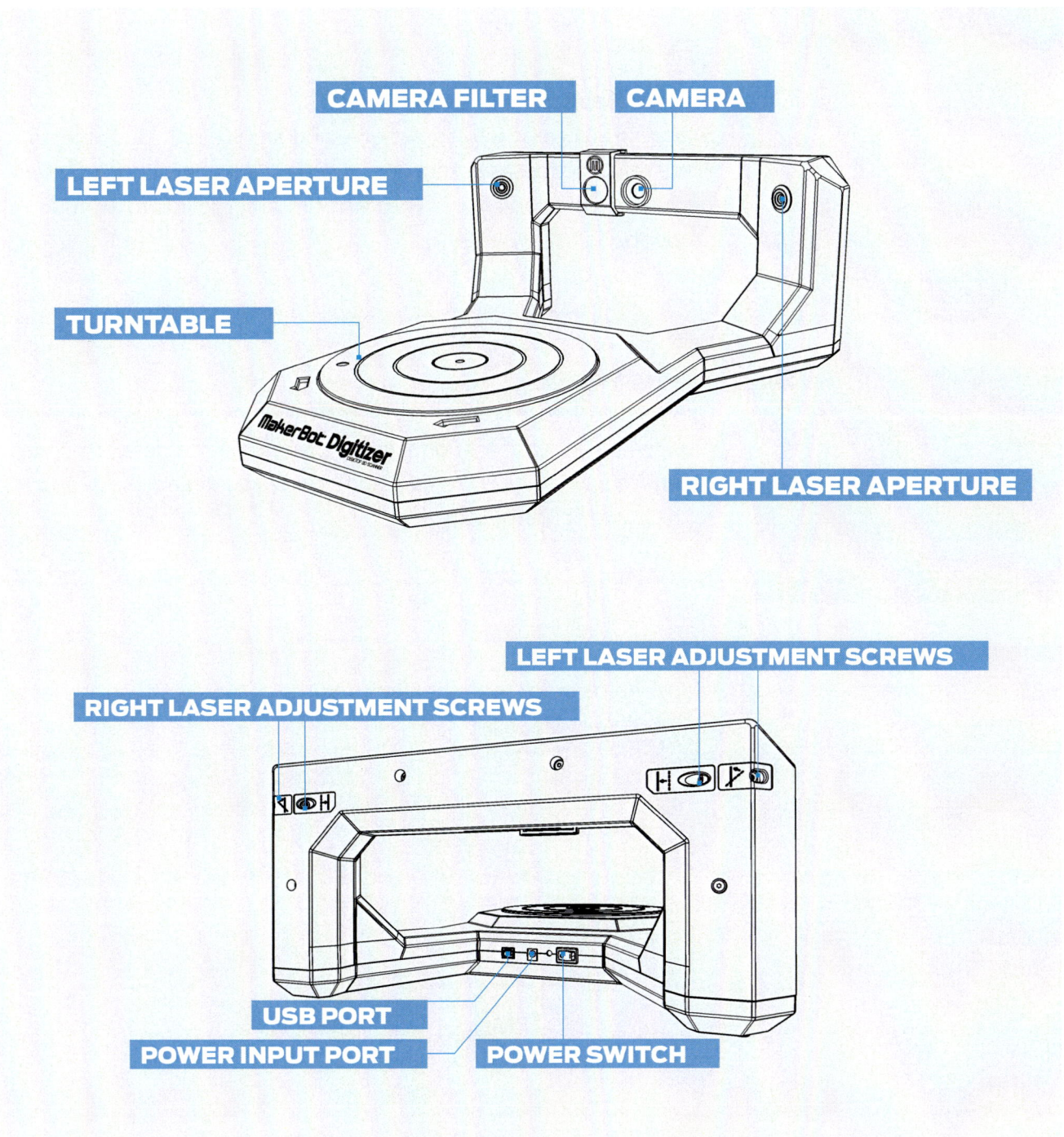

WHAT CAN I DO WITH A 3D SCAN?

A scan of a real-world object can be a great starting point for a new 3D design. Rescale, modify, and remix your scan as you see fit. Then print!

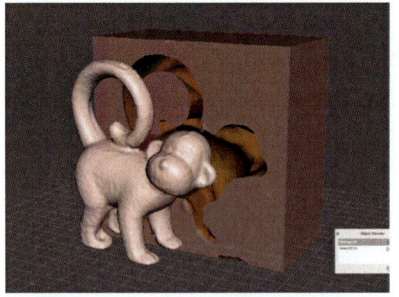

Scan as a Reference
Consider using the scan to build custom packaging or a stand to go along with your object. Sculpt something out of clay and create a custom mold you can use repeatedly.

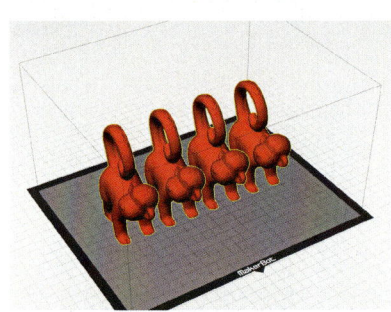

Scan to Replicate
Scanning is a great way to preserve and archive precious objects. Have valuable fossils or museum pieces? Consider scanning them to make digital copies that you can print and provide to all your students.

Scan to Modify
Use a scan as your starting point and modify as you desire. Make a sculptural object functional or simply add back a detail that was altered. It's a great way to take something you already have and remix it into something new.

SETUP
Slide the filter over the camera. The filter helps block out other lights so the camera can see the laser.

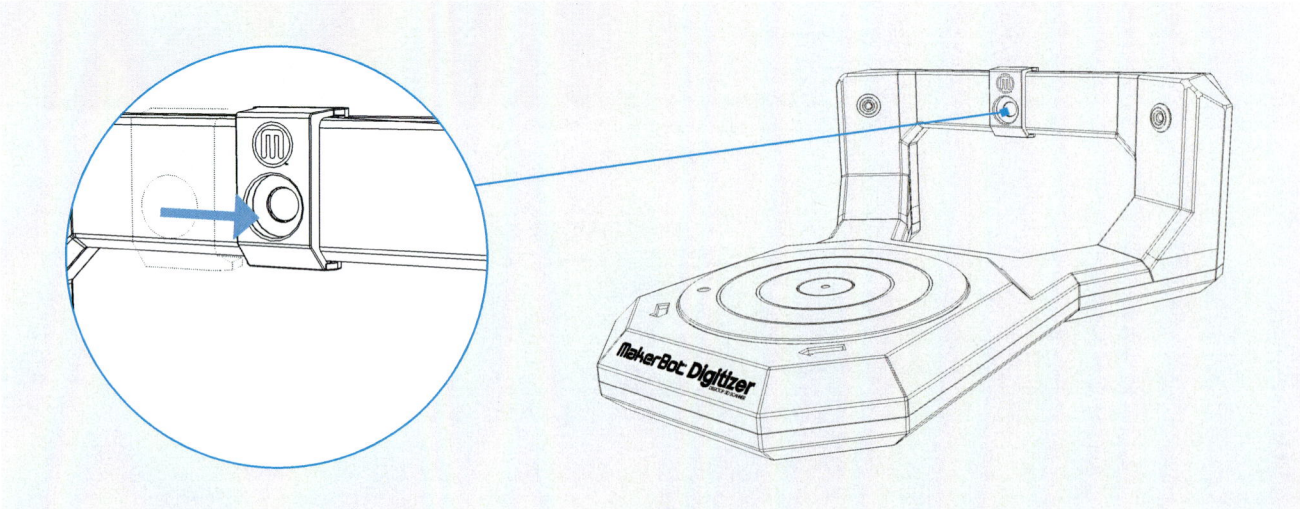

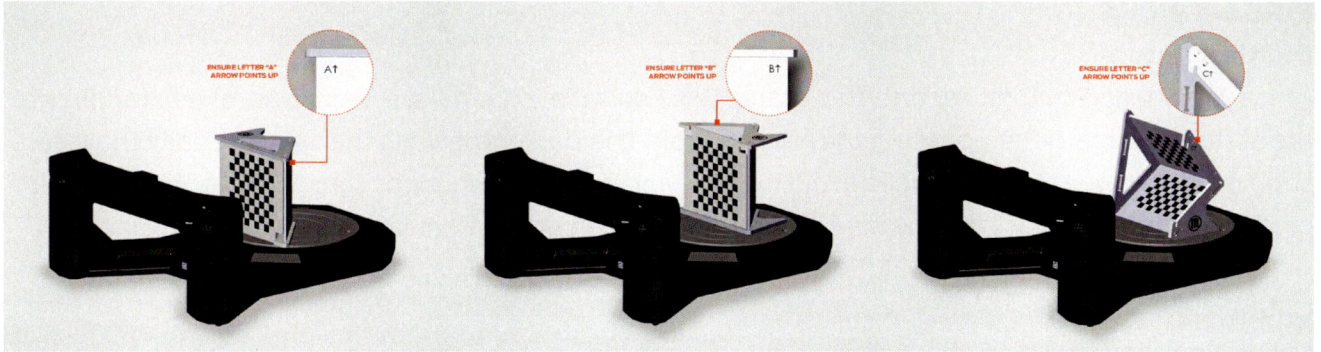

Calibration Tool A
Calibrate the camera. Using the calibration tool, find the side that has an A. Place the tab in the hole at the center of the turntable and let the script run. This process helps the program make adjustments for lens distortion.

Calibration Tool B
Calibrate the turntable. Now flip over the calibration tool to the side with the B up. Place the tab in the hole at the center of the turntable. As the script runs, the program is calibrating for the physical space in which the scan will take place.

Calibration Tool C
Calibrate the lasers. Finally, flip the calibration tool to the side with the C up. Slide out the middle plate on the tool and place it on the center of the turntable. In this step, the program is seeing where the lasers are in the scanning space.

Select the shade of the object within MakerWare for Digitizer. Evaluate your object to determine the proper shade category. Lighter objects are easier to scan and darker are more challenging.
Light: An object that's white or cream with little to no gloss
Medium: An object that's painted or gray with little to no gloss
Dark/Difficult: An object that's dark, glossy, fuzzy, or transparent. You might need to coat these objects with white powder before scanning.

TIPS & TRICKS

Digitizer Setup

Place your MakerBot Digitizer on a flat, stable work surface, and make sure no part of it extends over the surface's edge. Set it up facing the nearest wall. The darker the wall, the better. Ideally the lasers should point toward the wall while avoiding any windows or other bright light sources. Bright direct or reflected light shining in the camera can interfere with your scan, causing extra objects to show up.

Calibration

Calibration ensures the positions of the turntable and lasers are recorded accurately so your MakerBot Digitizer can produce the best possible scans. The only time you must have light is during the calibration routine. Avoid direct overhead light, though. If you must calibrate in a dark space, illuminate the calibration tool with a lamp or flashlight behind your scanner so it's not shining right into the camera.

Lighting

Scanning in low light is best. If you're having trouble scanning something with the Dark setting, try shutting off the lights completely. If you need to capture more detail, set the option to Dark/Difficult mode—even if the object is light colored. Be prepared for your scan to have some extra artifacts.

Hang black felt on the wall facing your MakerBot Digitizer to darken the wall's surface. That way any light in the room won't bounce off the background and cause bright spots the camera might misread as part of the laser line.

Other Considerations

How does object color affect scanning?
Dark objects cause the laser line to be partially absorbed by the object, making it harder for the camera to see. Visually, the laser line will appear dulled.

What can you do to help scan dark objects?
Coating the object in a lighter color before you scan it will help reduce laser absorption. Consider using something like baby powder, cornstarch, flour, or developer spray.

How does an object's translucency or texture affect scanning?
Shiny, translucent, or fuzzy objects can disrupt the camera from seeing the laser line because the laser will reflect in many directions. In other words, potential chaos!

What can you do to help scan a shiny or fuzzy object?
Again, coating the object will help reduce laser reflection or absorption. You may want to consider painting these objects with something matte like tempera paint.

Which of the following colors scan best? Which are difficult to scan?
- Red – Best (red color reflects red light the best)
- White – Good
- Yellow – Okay
- Green – Most difficult (green color absorbs red light so it does not scan well)
- Blue – Difficult
- Purple – Difficult

What happens when there's sunlight in front of the camera? Behind the camera?
Sunlight directly in front of the camera makes it difficult for the camera to see the laser line. This often produces non-optimal scans. Sunlight behind the camera is better than in front but should be minimized so the camera can see the laser line.

What are practical applications for scanning?
Scanning is a great way to get a digital representation of an object. It can be used to preserve a model, use it as a reference, or modify it into a remixed version.

How can you modify a scan in a 3D modeling program?
Programs like Tinkercad, MeshMixer, and Sculptris are useful for importing and modifying scans.

Activity: Once you've calibrated, ask your students to find objects to scan in the classroom. Before scanning them, discuss as a class whether each will be a good object to scan or a difficult one. If the object is going to be difficult to scan, describe the steps you could take to make it more scannable. Do not be afraid to explore what's possible.

KNOWLEDGE CHECKS
- How does the MakerBot Digitizer work?
- What can you use 3D scans for?
- What are ideal scanning conditions?
- How can you use a MakerBot Digitizer in your classroom?
- Can you identify how to make your scans successful?

WAYS TO DESIGN

LEARNING OBJECTIVES
- Understand the different types of 3D modeling software
- Explore the differences among 3D modeling programs and their strengths and weaknesses

WHAT IS 3D MODELING?
3D modeling is the process of creating a digital representation of objects. Numerous 3D modeling software programs allow for the creation of 3D models in a variety of ways.

Just as pens, pencils, brushes, and clay are tools that you use in your creative process, 3D modeling programs are tools you can use in your digital design process. It's not about learning one right tool, but rather about finding the tool that fits your design the best. Explore a few 3D modeling programs and see which best fit your desired outcomes. In this section, you'll find ways to help you approach this process.

TERMINOLOGY
- **Mesh:** The collection of vertices, edges, and faces that defines the shape of a 3D model
- **Watertight:** A continuous outside surface (or **mesh**), necessary for successful 3D printing. For example, an object like a donut, even though it has a hole in the middle, has a continuous outside surface and could be 3D printed.
- **Transform:** A tool that allows a user to move or rotate an object's position
- **Viewport:** Specifies your window into the 3D modeling tool; in other words, the view you see on screen
- **Orbit:** Rotates your viewport around a point or object
- **Pan:** Moves your viewport up and down or left and right
- **Zoom:** Moves your viewport closer to or farther from a point in a scene
- **Perspective View:** Adjusts the point of view to match how the human eye sees. Objects that are further away appear smaller than objects that are closer to the camera.
- **Orthographic View:** Adjusts the point of view to a single perspective. All objects of the same size appear to be the same size, no matter their distance from the camera.

WHAT CAN I DO WITH 3D MODELING?

3D modeling gives you the freedom to design whatever you'd like. For inspiration and references, resources like Thingiverse and GrabCAD can be helpful; use them to find 3D models that other people have already designed. The thing you want to make might be best constructed by remixing a model or building off an existing design (license permitting). As you learn to model, consider uploading your files to Thingiverse and/or GrabCAD so you can to continue to grow and engage with the community, and so other people can remix and expand on what you've made.

3D MODELING SOFTWARE

There are a lot of different 3D modeling programs available, all with different strengths and weaknesses. Recently, many programs have launched that are both easy to use and free. In this book we'll focus mainly on these free programs. When looking at 3D modeling programs, you'll find that all of them fall into three major categories: solid modeling, digital sculpting, or polygon modeling.

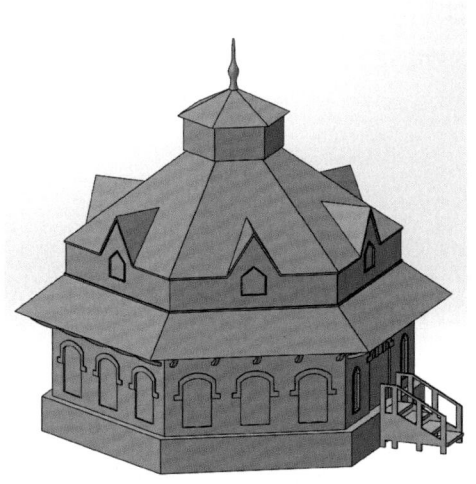

Solid Modeling

Solid modeling (or CAD) programs work well for creating models with real-world dimensions and are used to make functional parts. In some of the advanced programs you can form complex assemblies of objects, run simulations, and more.

- **Industries:** Engineering, industrial design, architecture
- **Free software:** Tinkercad, 123D Design, and more
- **Paid software:** Inventor, SolidWorks, Rhino, and more
- **Strengths:** Creating mechanical structures with dimension, building assemblies, simulating real-world physics, material property libraries, design history
- **Weaknesses:** Creating organic shapes, detailed surface textures and patterns

Digital Sculpting

Digital sculpting simulates the process of sculpting clay. You're able to push and pull this digital clay to create highly detailed and textured models. It works well for creating organic models such as faces, plants, etc.

- **Industries:** Film, video games, art
- **Free software:** Sculptris, SculptGL, and more
- **Paid software:** ZBrush, Mudbox, 3D-Coat, and more
- **Strengths:** Highly detailed models, organic shapes, digital painting
- **Weaknesses:** Creating functional parts is difficult, often requires peripherals (drawing tablet), steep learning curve for advanced programs

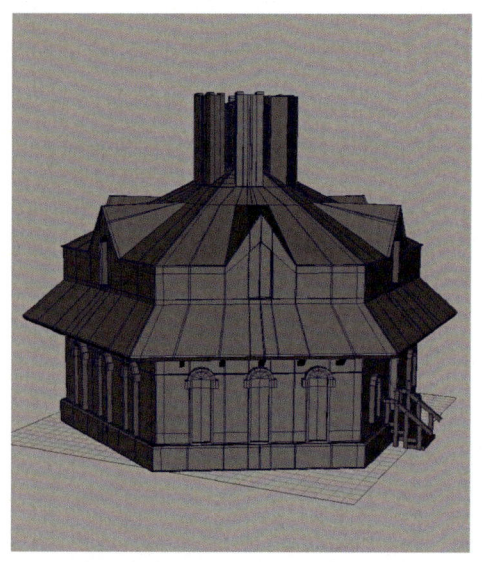

Polygon Modeling

Polygon modeling gives you direct control of the mesh, faces, vertices, or edges of a model. This allows you to create highly detailed and intricate 3D models. These models can be both organic and rigid.

- **Industries:** Animation, visualization, film, video games
- **Free software:** Blender, Wings 3D, and more
- **Paid software:** Maya, 3ds Max, Cinema 4D, and more
- **Strengths:** Can create highly detailed, intricate models; direct control of the mesh; preferred tool for animation
- **Weaknesses:** Because it's intended for on-screen environments, extra consideration must be taken while modeling for 3D printing

Programs for the Classroom: In the Projects section of this book, we'll be using Tinkercad, OpenSCAD, Sculptris, 123D Design, and MeshMixer. All of these programs are free. Learning the basics of each will give you a better understanding of their strengths so that, moving forward, you can determine the best tool for your projects.

GETTING STARTED IN 3D MODELING

There are a variety of ways to approach learning 3D modeling, and over time you'll develop your own style, techniques, and preferences. Below you'll find some techniques that focus on helping you take that first step, regardless of where you choose to start.

Reference Objects/Images

One of the best ways to start is to find an object and use it as a reference. Thingiverse and GrabCAD are great places to get inspiration and download reference objects. Objects you have around you are another great resource. Pick an object from your classroom, take a look at it, and start to imagine how you would recreate it. Is there any way you could break it down into smaller, simpler parts?

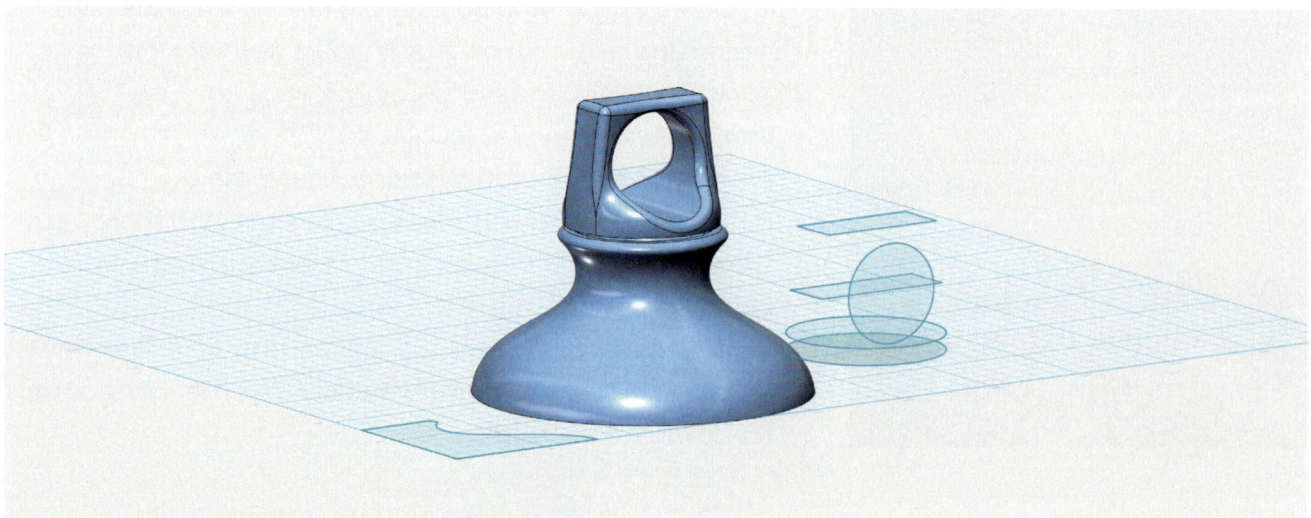

Here we recreated the top of an aluminum water bottle.

Primitive Building

Learning how to 3D model is similar to learning how to draw. Beginners should start with large, simple shapes and then refine the details. These shapes are referred to as primitives in most 3D modeling programs. Primitives are often composed of boxes, cylinders, and spheres, and can be modified and assembled to make complex models.

Activity: Pick an object in your classroom to be your reference. Study the object. What **primitives** could you use to recreate the basic shape of that object? This process is second nature to experienced designers. When exploring Tinkercad later on in this book, you'll see the importance of breaking down objects into simple shapes.

Navigation vs. Transformation

The next step to approaching 3D modeling is to learn how to move objects around versus moving your camera's view in your program of choice.

In 3D modeling programs, your view acts as a camera, exploring objects from different angles within your workspace. In the same way that you would move a camera in the real world to find different frames for shots, you can use the program to look around your objects from a variety of different vantage points. This is referred to **navigating** the scene.

When you want to change the position of an object in your workspace, you're **transforming** it. In the real world, this compares to physically picking up an object and moving it around or rotating it.

Picture an apple sitting on your desk. If you wanted to see the other side of the apple, you could either pick the apple up and turn it around (**transforming**) or stand up and walk around your desk until you see the other side (**navigating**).

Activity: Have your students grab an object near them and place it on a table or desk.
- **Navigation**
  - **Orbit:** Ask the students what they would do if they wanted to see the other side of the object. Based on what they do, ask them if it's navigating or transforming.
    - Physically walking around the object to see it from a different side is called **orbiting** the scene, one form of **navigation**.
  - Picking the object up is a form of **transformation**.
  - **Zoom:** Ask the students what they would do in the real world if they wanted to get a closer look at the object. Based on what they do, ask them if it's navigating or transforming.
    - Physically getting closer to the object is called **zooming**, another form of navigation.
  - **Pan:** While the students are close to the object, place another object outside of their field of vision. Ask them what they would do if they wanted to see that object while remaining where they are.
    - Physically rotating your view is referred to as **panning** the scene, the third major form of navigation.
- **Transformation**
  - **Move:** Ask the students to physically move one of the objects on top of another. Ask them if it's navigating or transforming.
    - **Moving** is a type of transformation.
  - **Rotate:** Ask the students to physically turn the objects on their sides. Ask them if it's navigating or transforming.
    - **Rotating** is another form of transformation.

> TIPS: THESE ARE GREAT TOOLS TO HAVE AROUND WHEN YOU START ANY 3D MODELING PROJECT: NOTEPAD, GRAPH PAPER, DRAWING UTENSIL, DIGITAL CALIPERS, RULER, CALCULATOR, GRAM SCALE.

KNOWLEDGE CHECKS
- What types of 3D modeling programs are out there? Why would you want to use one over the other?
- What's the difference between navigating and transforming in 3D space?
- What are some of the ways to approach building 3D models?

CONCLUSION
The most important thing to remember when getting started with 3D printing is to take the first step. It doesn't matter if that step is to download and print a model from Thingiverse, scan and print your favorite souvenir, or design and print your own dream house. There are many options available. Choose one and dive in!

PROJECTS AND DESIGN SOFTWARE

In the following section, you will find four sample projects built with the intention of integrating 3D printing into the classroom.

Each of these projects uses a different free 3D modeling software (Tinkercad, OpenSCAD, Sculptris, and 123D Design) so that you can explore the strengths of each. The intent of these projects is to discover the types of modeling software out there and how they might relate to subjects covered in your classroom. As you will learn after completing these projects, there is never just one solution to creating your own 3D models. By learning the strengths and weaknesses of the tools available to you, you will be able to decide which tool is best for any given project.

The sample projects are merely ideas to help you brainstorm ways to integrate 3D printing into your lessons. We do not expect these projects to fit every class perfectly; we aim to provide a reference for you as you work to build out your own 3D printing projects. We encourage you to try each of these projects to discover the pace and flow. How could you expand or contract the project based on your classroom goals and timelines? We ask that you take the knowledge you gain from exploring these sample projects and apply it to creating unique projects of your own.

As you build and modify these projects, consider sharing your ideas back with the 3D printing community on Thingiverse.

PROJECT: PRIMITIVE MODELING WITH TINKERCAD

MAKE YOUR OWN COUNTRY

BACKGROUND
In this project, you and your students will learn how to use a free program called Tinkercad. Tinkercad is a friendly and approachable program for getting started with 3D design. It features a drag and drop interface that will help students understand the basics of 3D modeling.

The following section outlines how you could incorporate this project into your social studies units, specifically those centered around geography and colonialism. We'll look at how you can design basic geographical tiles to represent various environments. Explore using 3D printing to create many small pieces that can be assembled into a larger object. Even if you don't have these specific units in your curriculum, Tinkercad will help you quickly jump in and make 3D models for any subject.

SCOPE
Your students will take on the role of being a new world explorer. They'll participate in creating 3D printed biome tiles that can be assembled into a new and uncharted territory. Once the tiles are assembled, the students can break into groups and develop settlements by surveying the land and discovering its natural resources. Supply and demand can be simulated by encouraging the groups to engage in trade with their neighbors. There are many factors that go into setting up a new town in a new world. This project can easily scale up or down to adapt to student numbers, grade level, time, subject matter, and resources available.

PROJECT OUTLINE
Investigate: Geography and Climates
Explore: Modeling with TinkerCAD
Create: Design a Water Tile
Create: Design a Forest Tile
Create: Design a Mountain Tile
Create: Design Your Own Land Tiles
Further Activities: Explore Your New World

LOGISTICS
It's recommended that students work in groups for the Investigate portion of the project, and individually during the Create portions.

- Technology
  - MakerBot Replicator
  - Computers with a WebGL-enabled browser (for example, Google Chrome or Mozilla Firefox) and MakerBot Desktop installed
  - Three-button mouse (optional)
- Suggested print time: 20–30 minutes per tile
- Suggested model size: 30 mm x 30 mm per tile
- Suggested number of prints: one or two per student
- Visit www.tinkercad.com to create an account(s).
  - You can set up one free account for your whole class or, if possible, have each student create their own free account.

Note: Because Tinkercad runs in an internet browser instead of locally, disruptions in wireless or networked internet access, as well as server problems at Tinkercad, could cause a disruption to your class schedule. It's a good idea to always have a backup plan when working with Tinkercad.

LEARNING OBJECTIVES

General
- Explore the history of colonialism
- Research the geography of different regions
- Understand the importance of natural resources
- Learn basic principles of economics (supply and demand)
- Create 3D printed visuals for the classroom

3D Printing
- Building in pieces
- Optimizing print time
- Printing multiple objects at a time

3D Design (Primitive Modeling)
- Navigation
- Shape Generators
- Primitives
- Holes

TERMINOLOGY
- **Primitive**: A basic 3D geometric shape
- **Terrain**: A stretch of land with focus on its physical features
- **Hotkey**: A keyboard shortcut to a tool
- **Group**: Combining primitives into one shape
- **Hole**: A primitive that removes material when grouped with other objects

EXPLORE: PRIMITIVE MODELING WITH TINKERCAD

Tinkercad is a browser-based program that requires an account to sign in. According to its developers, it will work best on Firefox or Chrome. You can set up a class account and distribute the password. Once everyone is signed in, click the blue **Create new design** button.

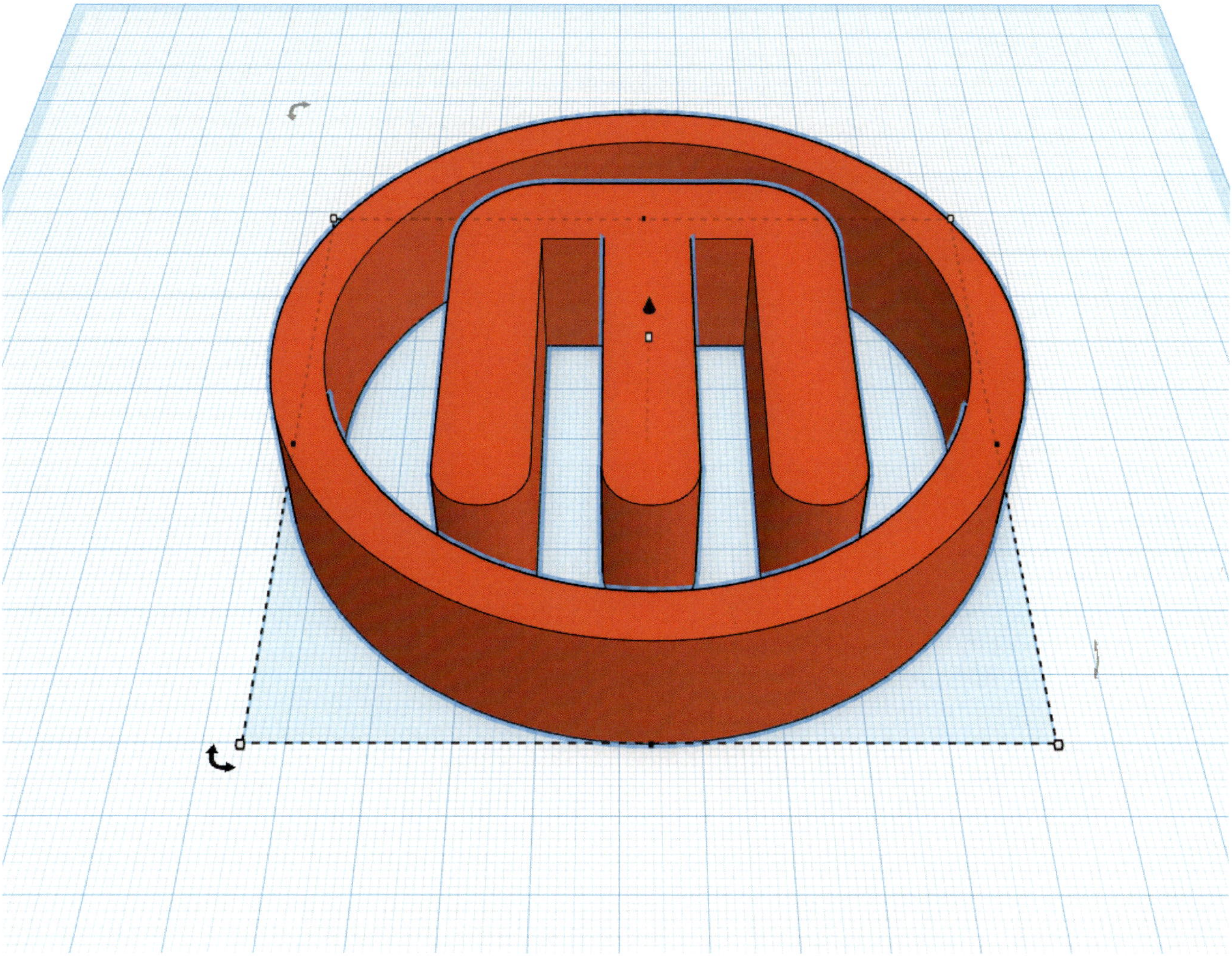

INTERFACE

The following elements of the interface should look like the image below.

1. **Workplane** – Blue grid surface where you'll build your models
2. **Camera navigation buttons** – Use these to navigate around your Workplane or use the mouse shortcuts described below
3. **System options** – Save your design, edit properties, and access help topics
4. **File name** – Notice that Tinkercad will automatically give your project a crazy name; you'll be able to change that later if you wish
5. **Action buttons** – Undo/redo actions and modify your design by grouping or aligning objects
6. **Primitives menu** – Long column of menus containing lots of modeling tools; you'll use these primitives to build your models
7. **Grid options** – Change the size of your Workplane and the snap interval value

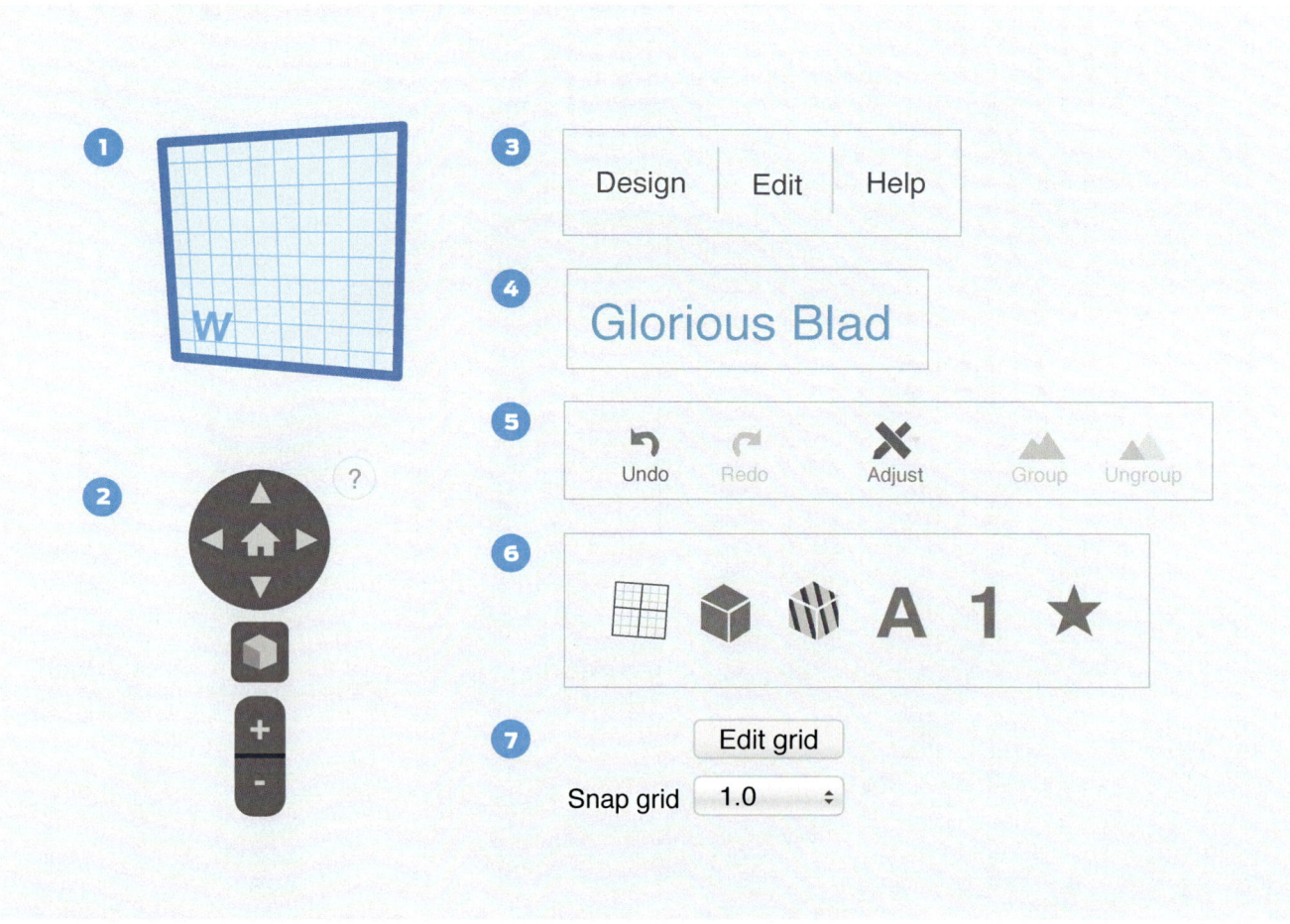

STEP 1: PLACE OBJECTS ON THE WORKPLANE.
Let's start by dragging and dropping to add some objects to our design.
- In the **Primitives** menu, scroll down until you see **Geometric**. You should see objects like **Box**, **Cylinder**, and **Pyramid**. If the triangle points right, it means the section is closed. Just click on the triangle to open it.
- Scroll up and down the Primitives menu and drag interesting things onto the **Workplane**.

STEP 2: LEARN HOW TO NAVIGATE.
You can move around in Tinkercad by pressing the navigation buttons in the upper left corner. With a three-button mouse, you can also use these shortcuts to become a navigation pro:
- Orbit – *Left-click and drag* to turn around the model.
- Pan – *Hold Shift key, right-click and drag* to move the Workplane around.
- Zoom – *Scroll the mouse wheel* up and down.

TIPS: THE VIEW WINDOW IS EASIER TO MANIPULATE WITH A THREE-BUTTON MOUSE THAN WITH A TOUCH PAD. USE THE HOME ICON TO RESET YOUR VIEW IF YOU GET LOST WHILE NAVIGATING.

STEP 3: MOVE AND RESIZE OBJECTS.
- Drag a red box primitive onto the Workplane. Orbit and/or pan your view as necessary to view the box from different angles.
- To move the box up or down, drag the black handle above the box.
- Experiment with the ways you can resize the box by clicking and dragging the small white and black boxes along its perimeter.
- To preserve the proportions of an object, hold down the Shift key when resizing. Now you can make an object bigger or smaller without changing its overall shape.

TIP: TINKERCAD ALSO HAS BUILT-IN TUTORIALS THAT YOU CAN USE TO EXPLORE MORE FEATURES AND TECHNIQUES.

STEP 4: USE THE RULER TOOL.

- The **Ruler** is one of the most important tools in Tinkercad. You can find it in the Primitives menu under **Helpers**.
- Drag the Ruler to any place on the Workplane.
- When the Ruler is on the Workplane, clicking on an object will also reveal its position and size values in each direction. You can modify the position or size of an object by clicking on the numbers and typing in values directly. This is useful when you need an object to be a specific size.

TIP: PRESS R ON YOUR KEYBOARD TO QUICKLY PLACE THE RULER. IT WORKS THE SAME WAY NO MATTER WHERE YOU PUT IT, SO YOU MIGHT WANT TO PLACE IT IN A FAR CORNER SO IT DOESN'T CLUTTER UP YOUR OBJECTS.

Start designing something simple then make your designs more and more complicated.

STEP 5: HAVE FUN AND MAKE SOME RANDOM THINGS!

A great way to learn Tinkercad is by experimenting. In this step you'll have time to explore and experiment while practicing the tools and menus within Tinkercad.

- Add things, move them around, have some fun. Experiment and see what happens.
- Experiment with the **Adjust**, **Align**, and **Mirror** tools.
- Here are a few ideas of basic shapes to try and build using primitives:
  - A house, a tree, or a road
  - A car, a boat, a bike, or a skateboard
  - A robot, a monster, a person, or a cat
  - A face, a joke, a frog, a hat, or anything you want

INVESTIGATE: GEOGRAPHY AND CLIMATES

TO INTEGRATE THIS PROJECT INTO YOUR CLASSROOM CONSIDER HAVING YOUR STUDENTS RESEARCH THE DIFFERENT BIOMES (DESERT, RAINFOREST, TUNDRA, ETC.), EITHER IN PAIRED GROUPS OR INDIVIDUALLY.

- What defines the biomes?
- Where are these biomes located?
- What makes each biome difficult to live in?
- What resources are abundant in each of the biomes?

HAVE AN OPEN DISCUSSION ABOUT THE RESOURCES YOUR STUDENTS USE DAILY. A RESOURCE IS A SUPPLY FROM WHICH BENEFIT IS PRODUCED.

- Have the students write down their favorite resource, and have them explain why.
- Have the students research which resources come from which biomes.

THE STUDENTS SHOULD RESEARCH HOW PEOPLE USE THESE BIOMES.

- What kinds of cultures live in each biome?
- How do residents grow or manage food?
- How are buildings made in response to living in these climates?

CREATE: DESIGN A WATER TILE

STEP 1: CREATE A TERRAIN TILE WITH A TERRAIN SHAPE GENERATOR.
The Create projects below will all be based on a **Shape Generator** object called **Terrain** (found in the **Primitives** menu). In this step we'll learn how to find and use Terrain to make a simple water tile like this one.

TIP: LIMIT THE HEIGHT OF THE WATER TILE TO 3 MM.

- Near the top of the **Primitives** menu is a category called **Shape Generators**. Open this category, and then open the subcategory **Community**. This menu contains special objects that were made by Tinkercad community members.
- At the bottom of the **Community** menu are a list of pages. Locate the **Terrain** tile. Drag the Terrain tile onto the **Workplane**.
- Drag the **Ruler** tool onto your Workplane. Resize your terrain tile by clicking on the dimensions and typing in new numbers so the tile measures **30 mm x 30 mm**. Press **Enter** to confirm.
- If you'd like to, you can color your water tile blue by selecting the tile and then using the **Color** option in the **Inspector** menu that appears in the upper right corner of the view area. Of course, your actual print color will depend on the color of filament in your 3D printer!
- When the terrain tile is selected, you should see the **Inspector** menu with three sliders that you can use to modify the shape of the terrain. Modify your tile until it looks like a slightly wavy piece of ocean. (We'll build more exciting tiles later!)
- To export this tile for 3D printing, go to the **Design** menu and select **Download for 3D Printing**. Press the **STL** button and wait for the design to begin downloading.
- Import the STL into MakerBot Desktop and prepare for printing. Print time should be roughly 20 minutes.

TIP: PLATE MULTIPLE TILES ON THE SAME BUILD PLATE SO THAT ALL OR MOST PRINTS ARE DONE BY THE NEXT CLASS PERIOD.

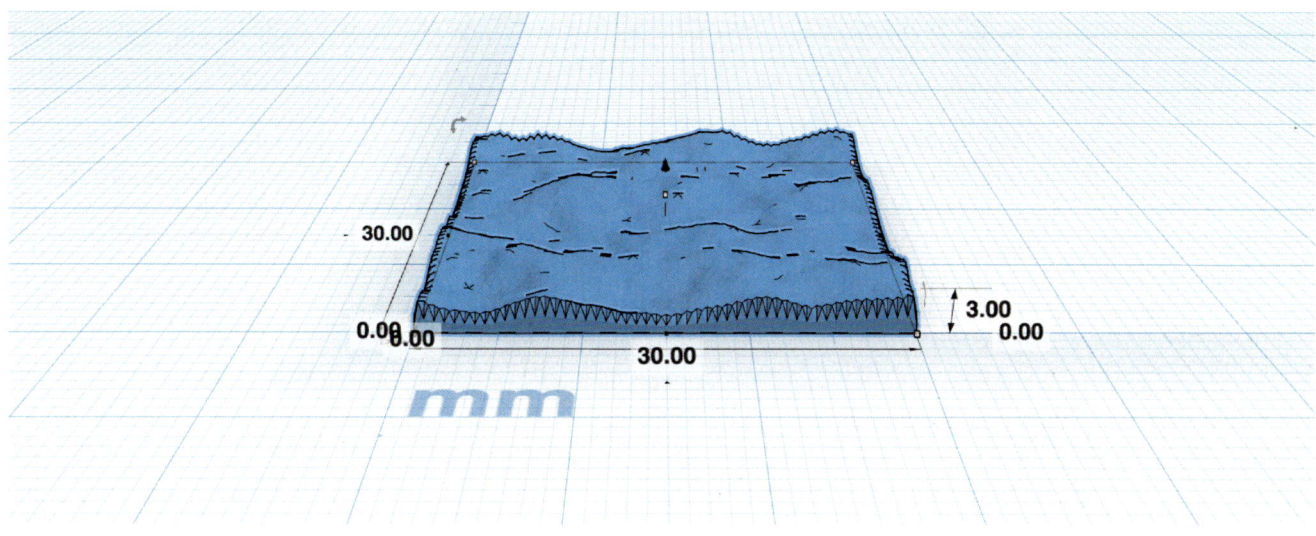

CREATE: DESIGN A FOREST TILE

In this project you'll modify your water tile to make a forest tile. Everyone's forest tile will look different, but the printed result might look something like the image below.

STEP 1: CREATE THE GROUND TERRAIN OF YOUR TILE.
- Make a copy of your **30 mm x 30 mm** water tile.
- Click on the tile and use the **Inspector menu** to adjust the terrain of the tile to your liking. Also adjust the height of your tile to make the terrain more dramatic. Will it be a hilly forest or a flat landscape? You decide.
- You might also want to change the color of your terrain from blue to green.

STEP 2: CREATE A TREE TRUNK AND A TREETOP.
The most important part of creating a forest tile is populating it with trees! In this step we'll set up the basic shapes that make up the tree.

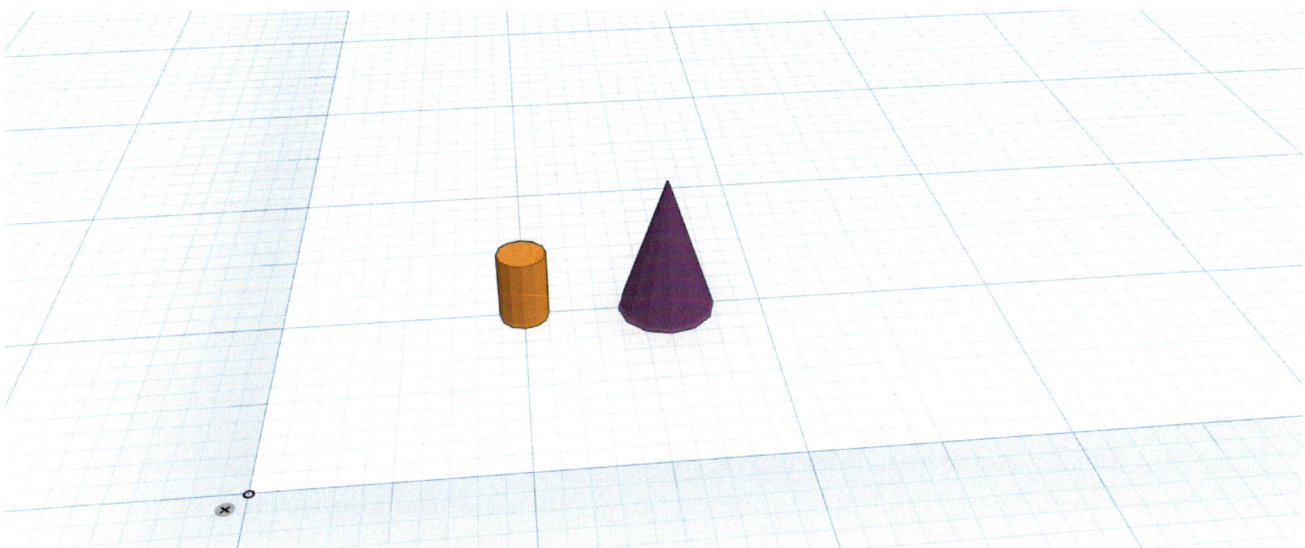

- Make sure you have the **Ruler** somewhere on the Workplane.
- Drag a **cylinder primitive** from the Geometric menu onto the **Workplane**.
- Resize the cylinder to **2 mm long**, **2 mm wide**, and **3 mm high**.
- Now repeat the same procedure to select and place a **cone primitive**.
- Resize the cone to **4 mm long**, **4 mm wide**, and **6 mm high**.
- Your Tinkercad design might now look something like this picture. Feel free to change the colors of your trunk and treetop as you like.

STEP 3: ALIGN AND GROUP THE TREE COMPONENTS.
Assembling your trunk and top into a tree requires a few new tools. If you make a mistake, use the **Undo button** and try again.

TIP: LIMIT THE HEIGHT OF THE FOREST TILE TO 10 MM.

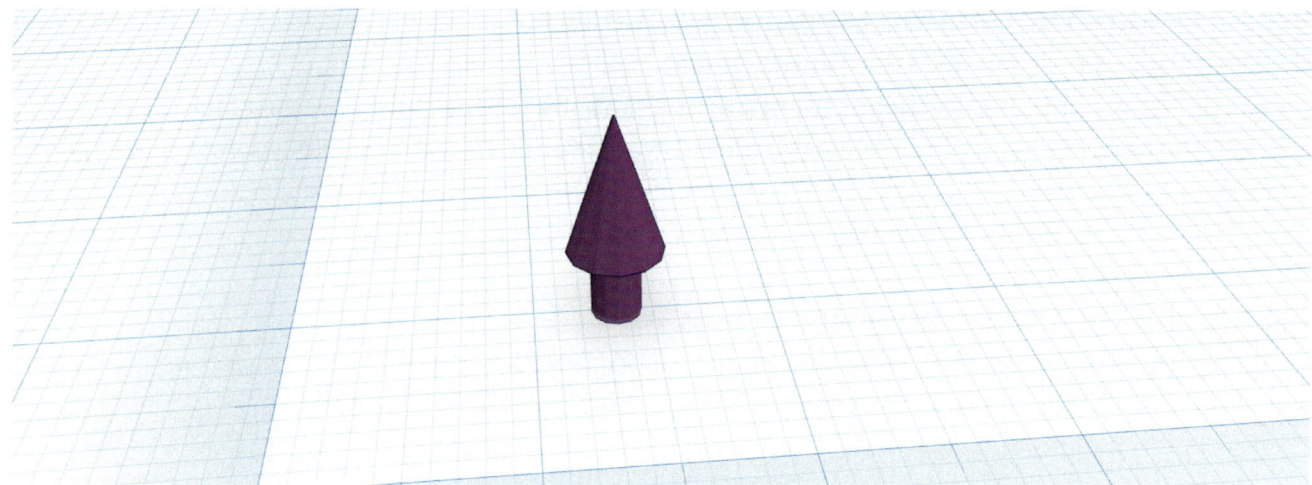

- Select the cone and look at its measurements. Drag the black handle on top of the cone and pull it upward **3 mm**, so it's at the same height as the top of the cylinder.
- Now you need to get the cone lined up directly over the cylinder. You can try to do this by moving the cone with the **mouse and/or arrow keys**, but it's much easier and more accurate to use Tinkercad's powerful **Align tool**. Select the **cylinder** and the **cone** at the same time by holding **Shift** and selecting both objects.
  - Click on the **Adjust** button in the top menu bar, and choose **Align** from the dropdown menu. You should see black pins around your two selected objects. These pins represent different possible alignment positions for the objects.
  - You want the **cone and the cylinder** to be **center-aligned** in both the **x-axis direction** and the **y-axis direction**. To do this, click on the center pin in the **x-axis direction** and the **center pin** in the **y-axis direction**. Your objects will snap into alignment.
- Now **group** the cylinder and cone objects together so they act as one combined unit. Make sure that both objects are still selected, and then press **Group** in the top menu bar.

STEP 4: PLACE AND SIZE YOUR TREE.
- Select and drag your tree onto the terrain tile. You can raise or lower the position of the tree with the black arrow handle above the tree.
- If you want to make your tree taller, shorter, wider, thinner, larger, or smaller, you can do so with the white and black handles around the tree object. For example, pull on the top white dot to stretch the tree taller, or pull out a corner dot to make the tree wider.

TIP: REMEMBER THAT YOU CAN **HOLD SHIFT** WHILE DRAGGING A CORNER IF YOU WANT TO MAKE THE ENTIRE TREE PROPORTIONALLY LARGER OR SMALLER WHILE KEEPING ITS SHAPE THE SAME.

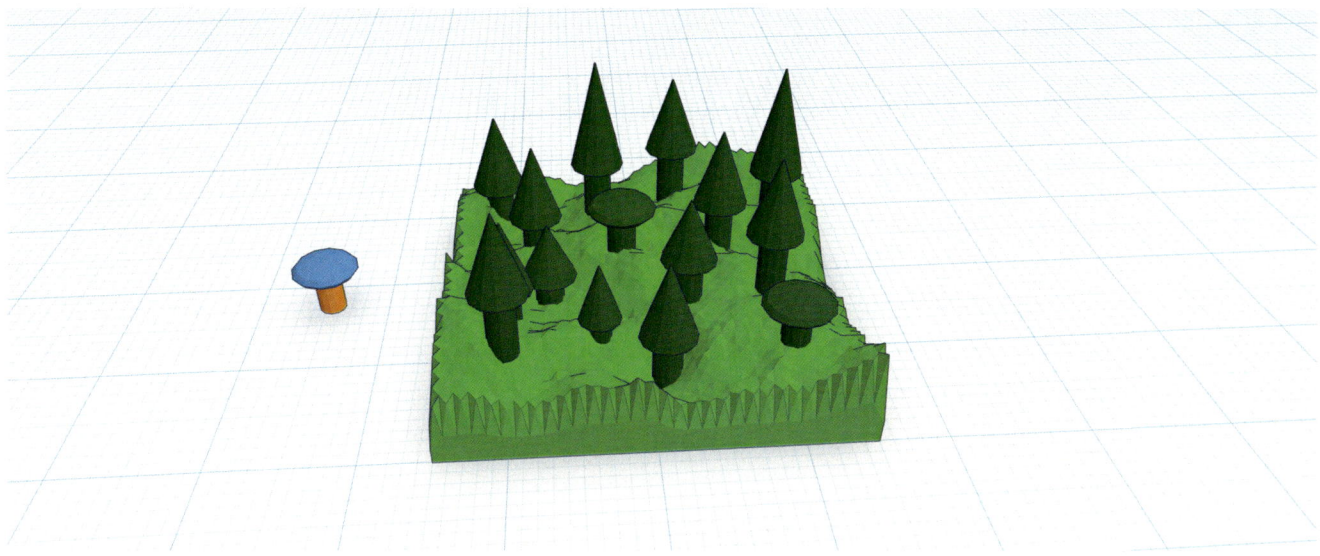

STEP 5: REPEAT TO MAKE A FOREST OF TREES.
To make an interesting forest tile, you'll need a lot of trees of different shapes and sizes. Use your creativity to make and place your own unique set of trees.
- Select your first tree and **copy/paste** to make a second one by using the **Edit** menu (or by using the **hotkeys** on your keyboard).
- Arrange your trees to make a small clustered forest, a large dense forest, or a sparse forest with room for a path, depending on what you like.
- Scale some trees up and down using the black and white squares around each object. Not all trees are the same in real life, so your forest may be more realistic if you vary the tree sizes. Make sure the trees don't exceed a height of **15 mm**, and the cylinder trunks don't get too thin or fragile.
- Try making a few different kinds of trees by experimenting with different geometric shapes for the treetops.
- When you're done with your forest tile, click and drag a selection window around all of its components and press **Group**. If you'd like to keep the multiple colors of your trees and landscape, click on **Color** in the **Inspector** window and select **Multicolor**. Of course, the color of your final 3D printed tile will be determined by the color of filament in your printer, not by the colors you choose in Tinkercad.
- Import the **STL** into **MakerBot Desktop** and prepare for printing.

CREATE:
DESIGN A MOUNTAIN TILE

In this project you'll use the design techniques you've learned so far to make a mountain tile. Along the way you'll learn about Tinkercad's **Hole** tool. Everyone's mountain tile will be unique, but yours might look something like the image below when you're done.

STEP 1: GENERATE A BASE TILE.
Let's start by making a base landscape. Later we can add more dramatic mountain ranges.
- Make a copy of your **30 mm x 30 mm** water tile.
- Click on the tile and use the **Inspector menu** to adjust the terrain of the tile to your liking.
- You might also want to change the color of your terrain from blue to yellow.

TIP: LIMIT THE HEIGHT OF THE BASE TILE TO **3 MM**. LIMIT THE HEIGHT TO **15 MM**.

STEP 2: CREATE SOME TALL MOUNTAIN RANGES.
In this step you'll add mountain ranges to your base tile.

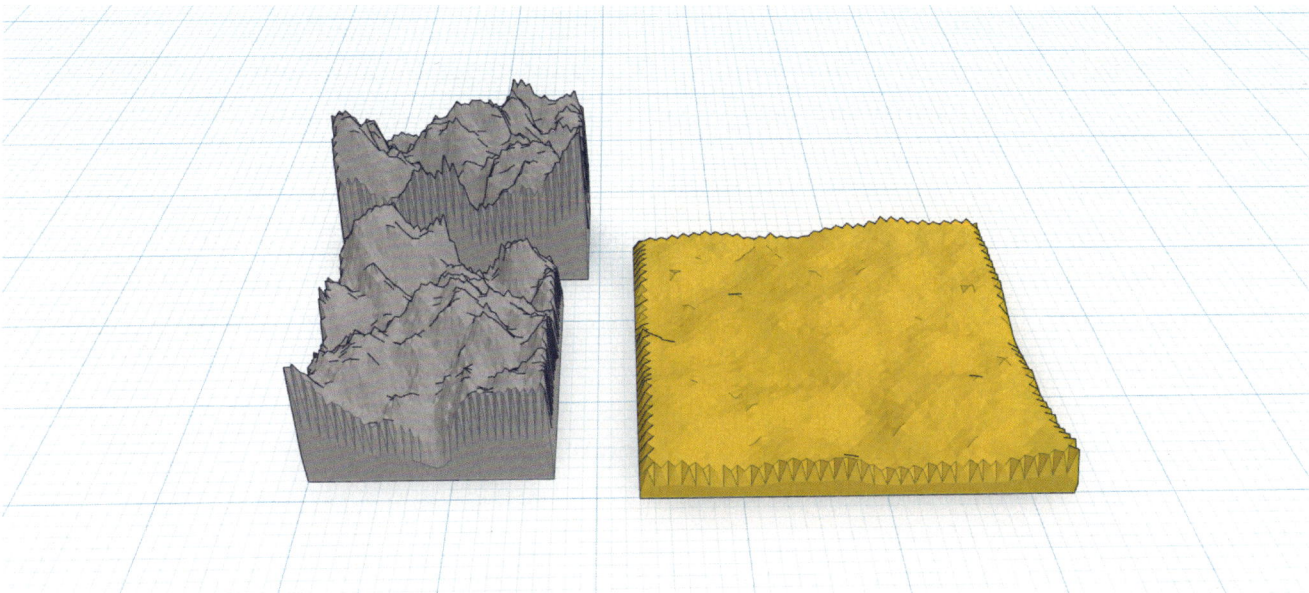

- Use an additional terrain tile to make a dramatic mountain range. Make the mountains taller by adjusting the height of the tile itself with the white square at the top of the object.
- Use additional terrain tiles to create a variety of mountain shapes.

STEP 3: ARRANGE THE MOUNTAIN RANGES ON YOUR TILE.
In this step you'll merge the mountain ranges you've created into your base tile.

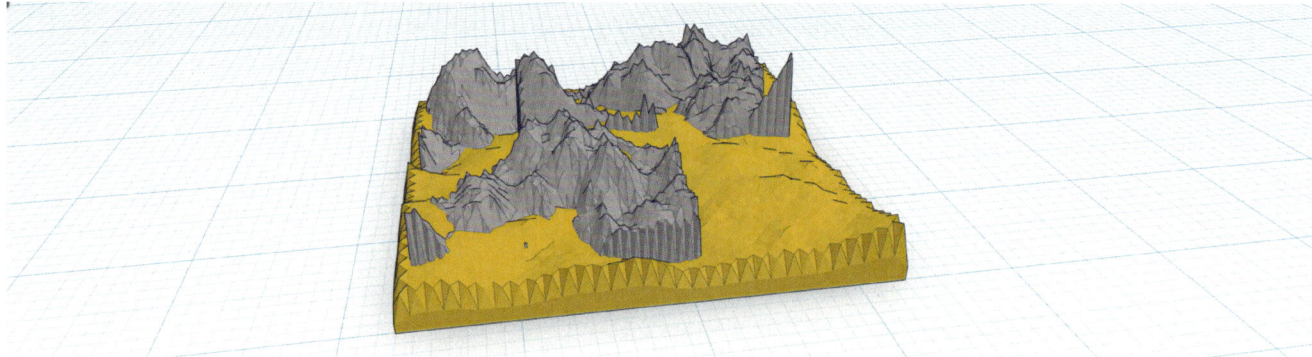

- Drag your mountain tiles onto the base and rotate or arrange them however you like.
- To make the transition between the mountains and the ground a bit more natural, select a mountain range and use the black handle above the object to push it down further into the base tile. This will make the bottom of the mountain range extend below the base tile, but that's okay; we'll cut that part off in the next step!

STEP 4: CUT OFF THE BOTTOM OF THE TILE USING THE HOLE TOOL.
One of the most powerful tools that Tinkercad offers is the ability to make some objects holes that cut away pieces of other objects. In this step you'll use that tool to cut off any stray pieces of mountain range that extend below your base tile.
- Orbit your view so that you can see underneath the base tile.
- Drag a cube from the **Primitives** menu onto the **Workplane**.
- Resize the cube so that it's comfortably larger than your base tile, and shift it downward so its top is exactly at the bottom of your tile.
- Select the cube and then click the **Hole** button in the **Inspector** menu.
- Select all objects and press **Group** to combine them. Notice that the hole will cut away from the rest of the object.

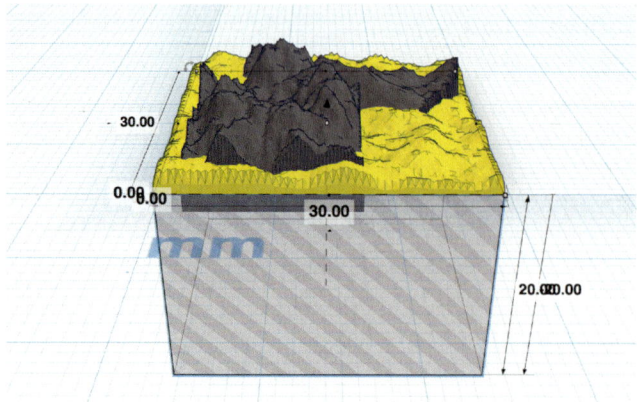

TIP: IF YOUR CUBE HEIGHT IS 50 MM THEN YOU CAN DO THIS BY SETTING THE DISTANCE BETWEEN THE BOTTOM OF THE CUBE AND THE WORKPLANE TO −50 MM.

CREATE: DESIGN A LAND TILE

Now use the techniques from the previous three Create sections to make your own land tile! On the next page you'll see some variations on the forest, water, and mountain tiles that we've designed.

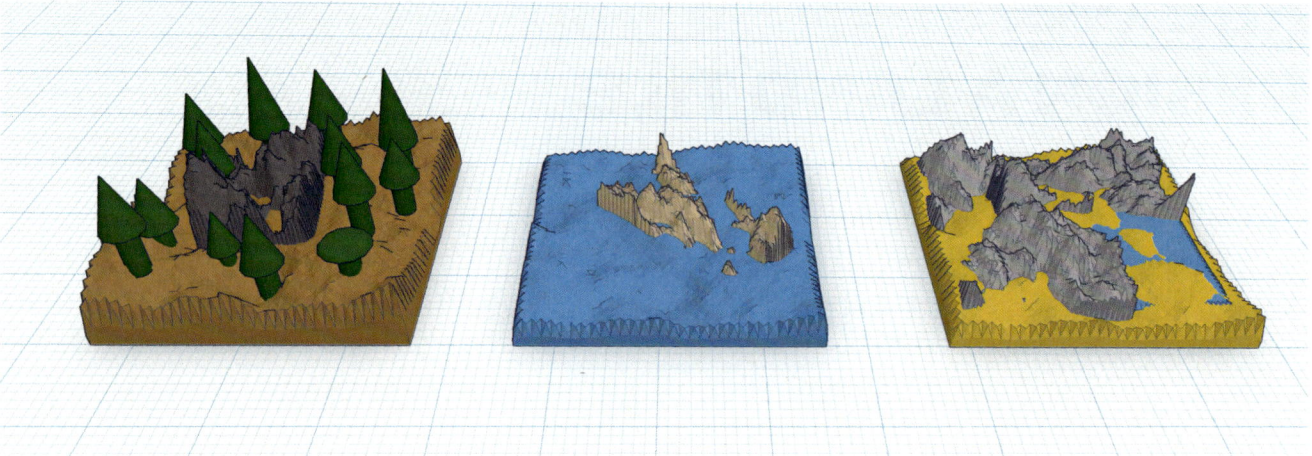

- Make a **30 mm x 30 mm** base tile with the **Terrain Shape Generator**. Randomize the shape of the terrain until it has the look you want, and make the land contours taller or shorter by stretching the tile itself from the top.
- Create land features to add to your tile. Try things from nature like hills, mountains, valleys, rivers, and trees. Or if you want to add man-made structures like bridges and houses, you can try that too! Just make sure your structures aren't so small that they won't print.
- Once the students have completed their designs, ask each to download one or two tiles and get them ready for 3D printing. To export this tile for 3D printing, go to the **Design** menu and select **Download for 3D Printing**. Press the **STL** button and wait for the design to begin downloading.
- Import the **STL** into **MakerBot Desktop** and prepare for printing. Print time should be roughly 20–40 minutes.

TIPS: PLATE MULTIPLE TILES ON THE SAME BUILD PLATE SO THAT ALL OR MOST TILES ARE DONE BY THE NEXT CLASS PERIOD. EACH CLIMATE COULD HAVE A FILAMENT COLOR THAT'S ASSOCIATED WITH IT. IF YOU WANT TO ADD EVEN MORE COLOR, TRY USING PAINT OR PAINT MARKERS TO DECORATE YOUR TILES AFTER PRINTING.

FURTHER ACTIVITIES: EXPLORE YOUR NEW WORLD

ACTIVITY 1: RESOURCES AND SETTLEMENTS

After you've modeled and printed everyone's tiles, assemble them on a large surface as a group. This 3D printed map will serve as the new world, established by your class.

Materials
- 3D printed land tiles
- Paint (optional)
- Large surface (for assembling map)

Steps
1. Have your students investigate and use their critical thinking skills to learn about historical settlements and how they were founded. Each student picks or is assigned a historical state, country, or place to research.
   - Investigate the geography and climate of the place.
   - Describe the natural resources of the area and how they were used.
   - Consider where the settlements were located and why they were built there.
   - Did the settlement have an economic system? What did it look like? Was there a currency?
   - Whom did the settlers trade with? What were they trading for?
   - Did they have any religious systems or cultural traits?

2. Following this research, break the students into teams. Give them the follow prompt: Your home country has sent your team on an expedition to discover and colonize new and uncharted lands. After sailing for many weeks on end, your fleet has spotted a new world and is landing to investigate.
   - Each team will pick a formation of 6–10+ tiles on the class map as its landing point.
   - Based on the location, the team will survey and establish a settlement in the region.
   - Using criteria similar to those in Step 1, have the teams compile information about their new settlements.
   - Have the students write a short description of their team's new settlement. They should take into consideration natural resources they get from each tile, and how they plan to set up their buildings and transportation.

ACTIVITY 2: CREATE TRANSPORTATION SYSTEMS
Now that you've established your settlement in your new world, it's time to think about how you're going to travel around. What would the transportation look like in your new environment?

Materials
- Computer with Tinkercad
- 3D printed tiles creating your class map

Steps
1. Have your students research traditional transportation systems, using history as a reference.
   - What are the benefits and drawbacks of each?
   - Are certain types of transportation specific to certain climates or geographies?

2. Have the teams brainstorm transportation systems for their settlements. What's the best way to travel the terrain? Roads, waterways, flying? The sky's the limit.
3. Have the students create these transportation systems in Tinkercad, either by modifying their original tiles or by modeling new parts to add to the existing class map. Perhaps they'll model a car, a hot air balloon, or a boat. Or maybe they'll invent a new type of transportation.

KNOWLEDGE CHECKS
- What are the benefits of modeling small, separate pieces for printing?
- What tools do you use to build objects in Tinkercad?
- What are the strengths and weaknesses of Tinkercad?
- How do you navigate in Tinkercad?
- When building the mountain tiles, why was it important to use the Hole tool to cut off the base of the tile?
- What are the benefits of plating multiple prints at a time?

MOVING FORWARD
Tinkercad is a great tool for getting started with 3D modeling. Despite the simplicity of its interface, Tinkercad is a very powerful tool, and many modelers have used it to create complex objects. In situations where you need to create a visual aid or prototype, Tinkercad can help you model an idea quickly and refine it further when needed. If you're not sure where or how to integrate 3D modeling into your subject, Tinkercad might be the tool for you.

PROJECT: PARAMETRIC MODELING WITH OPENSCAD

LEARN TO CODE FOR 3D PRINTING: MAKE A NAMETAG

BACKGROUND
In this project, students will learn and apply basic programming skills with the OpenSCAD language to style and customize a nametag. Visually, OpenSCAD is different from other types of 3D modeling programs. It's a simple declarative computer language that was built specifically for designing 3D printable models. By modifying existing OpenSCAD code for a wavy nametag, students will explore parameters, dimensions, "for" loops, translations, and boolean operations.

This project is suitable for all grades and ages, with no previous coding experience required. It can also be scaled up for more advanced students to explore the principles of geometry, trigonometry, and calculus.

SCOPE
Students will learn how to write basic code to generate objects with the OpenSCAD language. Once comfortable, they'll explore a sample coding project that prompts them to discover how changing different variables affects their 3D model. Finally, they'll add their own unique variables and functions to further customize a nametag.

PROJECT OUTLINE
Investigate: Parametric and Customizable Models
Explore: Modeling with OpenSCAD Code
Create: Customize a Nametag Using OpenSCAD Code
Create: Write OpenSCAD Code from Scratch to Design a Model
Further Activities: Customizer, Trigonometry, and Calculus

LOGISTICS
- Technology
  - MakerBot Replicator
- Suggested print time: 20–35 minutes per nametag
  - Computers with OpenSCAD and MakerBot Desktop installed
- Download OpenSCAD at www.openscad.org. This project requires OpenSCAD version 2015.03 or higher.
- Fully commented code for this lesson is in the file **MakerBot_NametagCode_Project.scad**, downloadable from the MakerBot Learning account on Thingiverse.

- For an easier variant of this project, or as a backup in case of local technology issues, the nametag design can be accessed from the MakerBot Learning account on Thingiverse. By selecting **Open in Customizer** from this link, the students can design their own nametags without having to interact with the code itself.

LEARNING OBJECTIVES
General
- Confidence writing basic code with simple parameters
- Understanding measurement and dimensions

3D Design (Parametric Modeling)
- Modifying parameters
- Basic OpenSCAD code
- Translation

TERMINOLOGY
- **Variable:** Symbol that signifies a value that can be fixed or changed depending on its definition
- **Function:** A body of code that returns a value or action
- **Parameter:** A variable within a set boundary
- **Facets:** Flat surfaces that make up the outside of an object. The more facets, the smoother the object.
- **Debug:** To search for and fix incorrect portions of code
- **Customizer:** Program built into Thingiverse.com that allows OpenSCAD files to be uploaded as user-editable models
- **Render:** To generate an output based on code written. In OpenSCAD, the render output is a solid object.

INVESTIGATE: PARAMETRIC AND CUSTOMIZABLE MODELS

One of the advantages of designing models with code is that you can make them **parametric**. This means you can have elements in your model that are easy to change, like the space between two parts or the length of a lever. The design process is all about iteration: you design something, try to print it in real life, learn from your model, redesign your model, and repeat. Parametric models help shorten the design process.

Before you get started with your own code, take a look at some of the customizable models on **Thingiverse**. Each customizable model was designed with OpenSCAD code that was then put into MakerBot Customizer, which provides an easy user interface for modifying parameters in the model.
- Go to **www.thingiverse.com**. Select the **Explore** tab and then choose **Customizable Things**. You'll see a wide variety of models that Thingiverse users have contributed.
- If desired, change the second category from **All** to another one, for example **Toys and Games**.
- Now choose something for the third category, for example, **Dice**. Many people have contributed models to **Thingiverse** for customizable dice! Choose one of the models, and once the model is open, press the button that says **Open in Customizer**.
- Within **Customizer**, you'll be able to modify whatever parameters the designer has made parametric, or changeable, in their model. Each model will have different parameters that will vary based on what the designer has enabled. Play around with **Customizer**; every time you choose or change a value on the left interface, the picture on the right will update to reflect your changes.
- You can also look at the code that the designer used to make their model by clicking on the **View Source** button that's under the picture of the model in **Customizer**. Some models are made with very complicated code, and some are surprisingly simple.
- Investigate two or three other customizable models of different types, changing parameters and peeking at the code for each one. There is great power, flexibility, and variety in designing with code. What would you design with this type of tool?

EXPLORE: MODELING WITH OPENSCAD CODE

When you open the OpenSCAD software, you'll see a window like the one shown. The basic workflow is to type code into the **editor window** on the left, press **F5 on a PC (or Function-F5 on a Mac)** to compile the code, and then look in the **view area window** on the right to see the result. A small **console log** at the bottom right will display output notes and sometimes error messages. You can use the mouse to navigate in the **view area**. Follow the steps in this section to get comfortable with how OpenSCAD works.

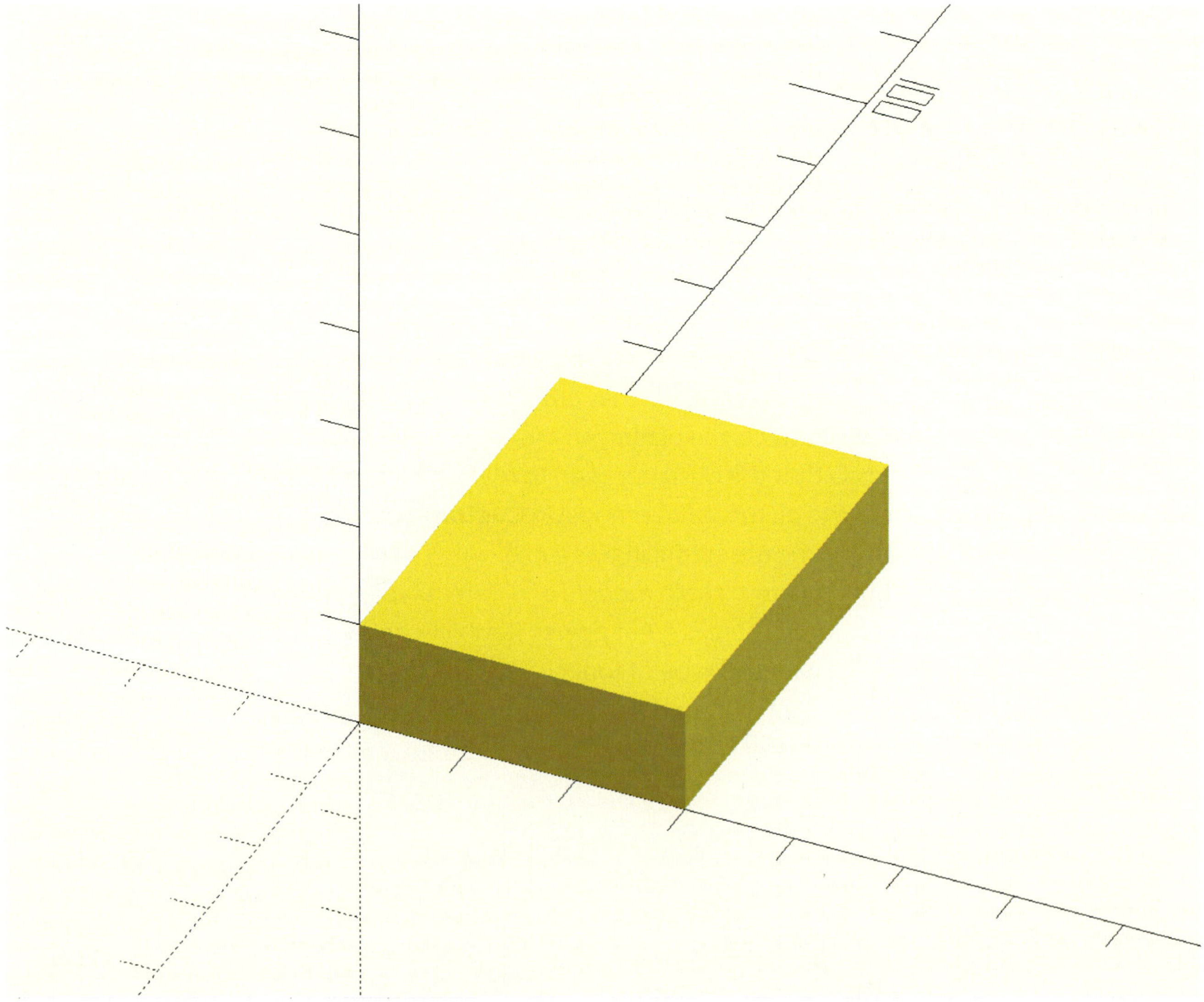

INTERFACE:
1. **Editor window** – Type code here to define your model
2. **System options** – Save your file, undo/redo actions, and format your code
3. **Model options** – **Preview**, **Render**, and **Export STL** files from this menu
4. **View area** – Displays the model defined in the editor window
5. **View menu** – Change your viewing angle using your mouse or the buttons in this menu
6. **Console** – Displays output notes and error messages

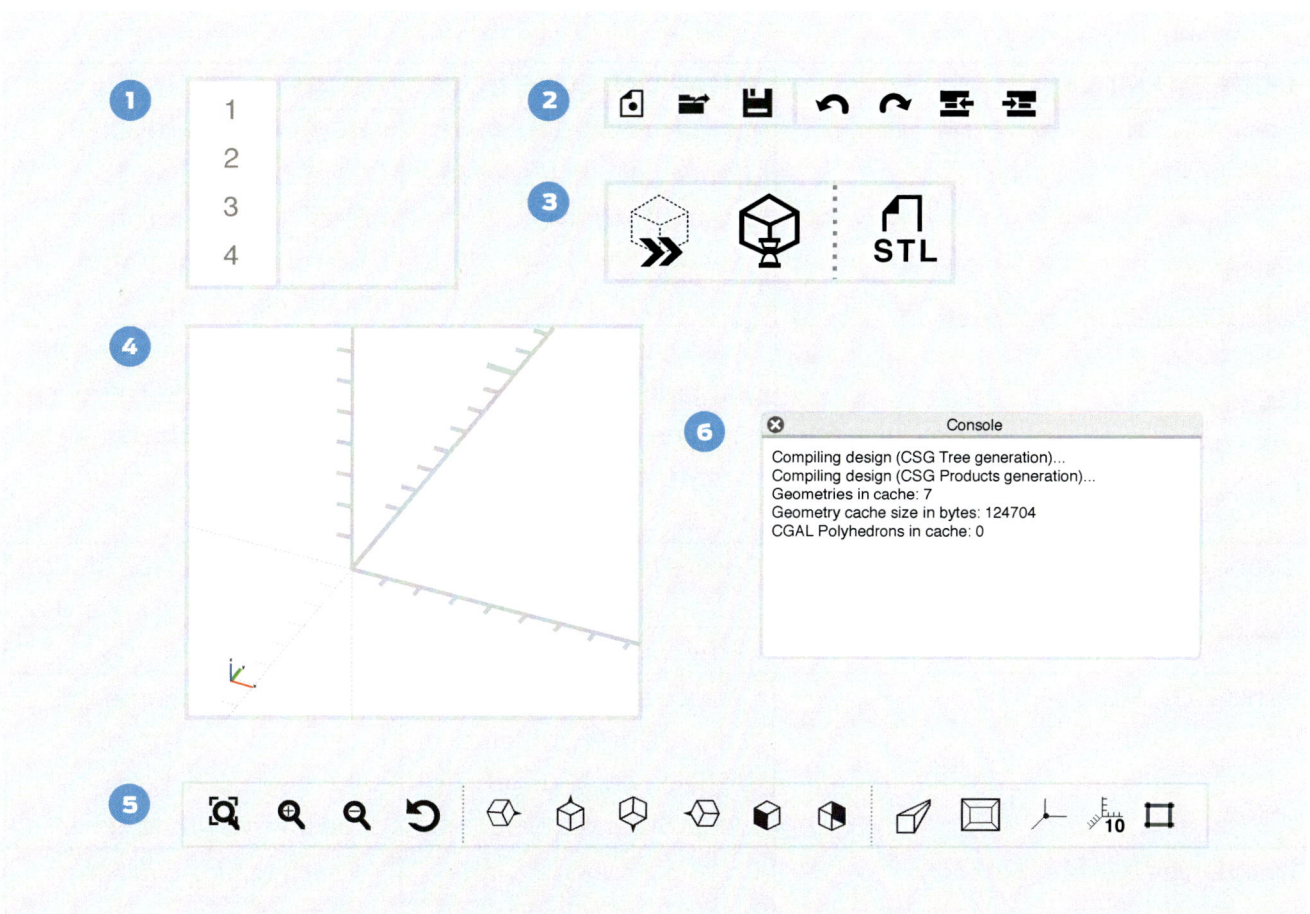

STEP 1: TYPE AND COMPILE YOUR FIRST OPENSCAD COMMAND
- Type **cube([30,40,10]);** in the editor window. Be sure to type it exactly as written.
- Press **F5** (or **Function-F5**) to see the resulting cuboid. As an alternative to using F5, you can use the **Preview** button in the **Model Options** menu.
- If your axes and/or scale markers are not visible, turn them on from the **View** menu.
- Notice that the cuboid is **30 mm** in the **x-direction**, **40 mm in the y-direction**, and **10 mm** the **z-direction**.

STEP 2: NAVIGATE AROUND THE OBJECT IN THE VIEW AREA.
- **Orbit** – *Left-click and drag* to orbit around the model.
- **Pan** – *Right-click and drag* to move the view around.
- **Zoom** – *Scroll the mouse wheel* up and down.

STEP 3: GET COMFORTABLE WITH BASIC OPENSCAD PRIMITIVES.
- Try typing the **primitives** commands in the table below into your OpenSCAD editor window and then press **F5** (or **Function-F5**) to see what happens.
- Experiment with modifying the code to get a feel for how the commands work.

CODE EXAMPLE	WHAT THE CODE DOES	NOTES
cube(30);	Creates a cube centered at the origin with all sides of length 30mm.	The semicolon tells OpenSCAD to draw the object. You'll need one at the end of many of your lines of code.
cube([30,40,10]);	Creates a cuboid with one of its corners at the origin and side lengths of 30 mm, 40 mm, and 10 mm.	The square brackets denote [x,y,z] coordinates. The round brackets (parentheses) pass information to the cube command.
cube([30,40,10], center=true);	Creates the same cuboid as above but with the center of the cube at the origin.	Sometimes one type of centering is more convenient than another.
sphere(20, $fn=24);	Creates a sphere with radius 20mm, centered at the origin, and with 24 facets around the equator.	Increasing the number of facets makes a smoother sphere, but can make your code take longer to compile.
cylinder(h=20, r=10, $fn=40);	Creates a cylinder with height 20mm and radius 10mm, centered at the origin, and with 40 facets around the equator.	Try setting $fn=6 or $fn=4; with a low number of facets so your cylinder can be a hexagonal or square prism.
cylinder(h=20, r1=10, r2=5);	Creates a truncated cone with height 20mm, lower radius 10mm, and upper radius 5mm, centered at the origin.	Note that when you don't specify $fn, OpenSCAD uses a default value.

STEP 4: GET COMFORTABLE WITH BASIC OPENSCAD MODIFIERS.

OpenSCAD also has commands for moving, scaling, extruding, and combining primitives. These are powerful tools for turning primitives into complete designs.

- Try typing the code snippets below into the **editor window**, and press **F5** (or **Function-F5**) to see what happens.
- Experiment with modifying the code to get a feel for what the commands can do.

CODE EXAMPLE	WHAT THE CODE DOES	NOTES
translate([-20,0,30]) cube(20, center=true);	Creates a 20mm cube centered at the origin, and then shifts the location of that cube −20 mm in the x-direction and 30 mm in the z-direction	The translate command modifies whatever primitive immediately follows it in the code. Note that translate itself doesn't get drawn, so it has no semicolon.
rotate(45, [0,1,0]) cube(20, center=true);	Creates a 20mm cube centered at the origin, and then rotates that cube 45 degrees around the y-axis (along the vector [0,1,0])	You may want to left-drag in the view area to look around the object and see how it was rotated.
linear_extrude(h=20) circle(20, $fn=6);	Creates a "circle" of radius 20 mm with only six facets (in other words, a hexagon), and then extrudes that shape upward for 20 mm.	Notice the use of the 2D primitive circle. The command linear_extrude only works on 2D objects.
linear_extrude(h=20, twist=60) circle(20, $fn=6);	Creates the same "hexagon-circle" with radius 20mm, and then extrudes that shape upwards for 20mm while rotating a total of 60 degrees.	The linear_extrude command is a modifier, not a primitive, so it does not need a semicolon.

difference(){
  cube(20, center=true);
  translate([0,0,-20])
    cylinder(h=50, r=8);
}
	Create a 20 mm cube and then remove a cylinder shape from it. The cylinder is translated downward so it penetrates through the cube.	The difference command draws the first object and then subtracts every other listed object from the first.

STEP 5: MAKE SIMPLE OBJECTS WITH OPENSCAD CODE.

Now use the code above to make some basic objects. See how many of the following objects you can make with OpenSCAD code. Remember to press **F5** (or **Function-F5**) after each update to your code so you can see the result.

- A 30 mm sphere that's shifted –10 mm in the x-direction, 40 mm in the y-direction, and 15 mm in the z-direction.
- A cuboid that measures 10 mm in the x-direction, 100 mm in the y-direction, and 5 mm in the z-direction.
- Two cylinders that intersect at right angles to each other.
- A pointy cone shape with another pointy cone shape underneath it in the opposite direction (like two ice-cream cones stuck together around their rims).
- A box with holes in each of its sides. You can use three cylinders to form the holes. Can you align the holes exactly to the center?
- An octagonal prism that twists 30 degrees from its base to its top.
- An open box with three small spheres inside it.
- A snowman!

STEP 6: EXPLORE MORE WITH ONLINE OPENSCAD TUTORIALS AND DOCUMENTATION.

- David Dobervich's *OpenSCAD Tutorial #1* video on YouTube
- Patrick Conner's *Welcome to OpenSCAD* video on YouTube
- OpenSCAD documentation, Cheat Sheet, and list of Getting Started Tutorials
  http://www.openscad.org/documentation.html

CREATE: CUSTOMIZE A NAME TAG USING OPENSCAD CODE

In this project, you'll design and 3D print a wavy-bordered nametag by modifying parameters in OpenSCAD code. You'll also dive into the code and learn how these parameters create the nametag design. Advanced students may want to change the code itself to create even more varied designs.

STEP 1: TRY TO FIGURE OUT WHAT THE CODE IS DOING.

Fully commented code for this lesson is downloadable from the MakerBot Learning account on Thingiverse.

Open the file **MakerBot_NametagCode_Project.scad** from MakerBot Learning on Thingiverse and look through the code in the **editor** window.

Don't type or change anything yet; just scroll through, look at the text, and try to figure out what might be going on in the code. The code should look something like the image below.

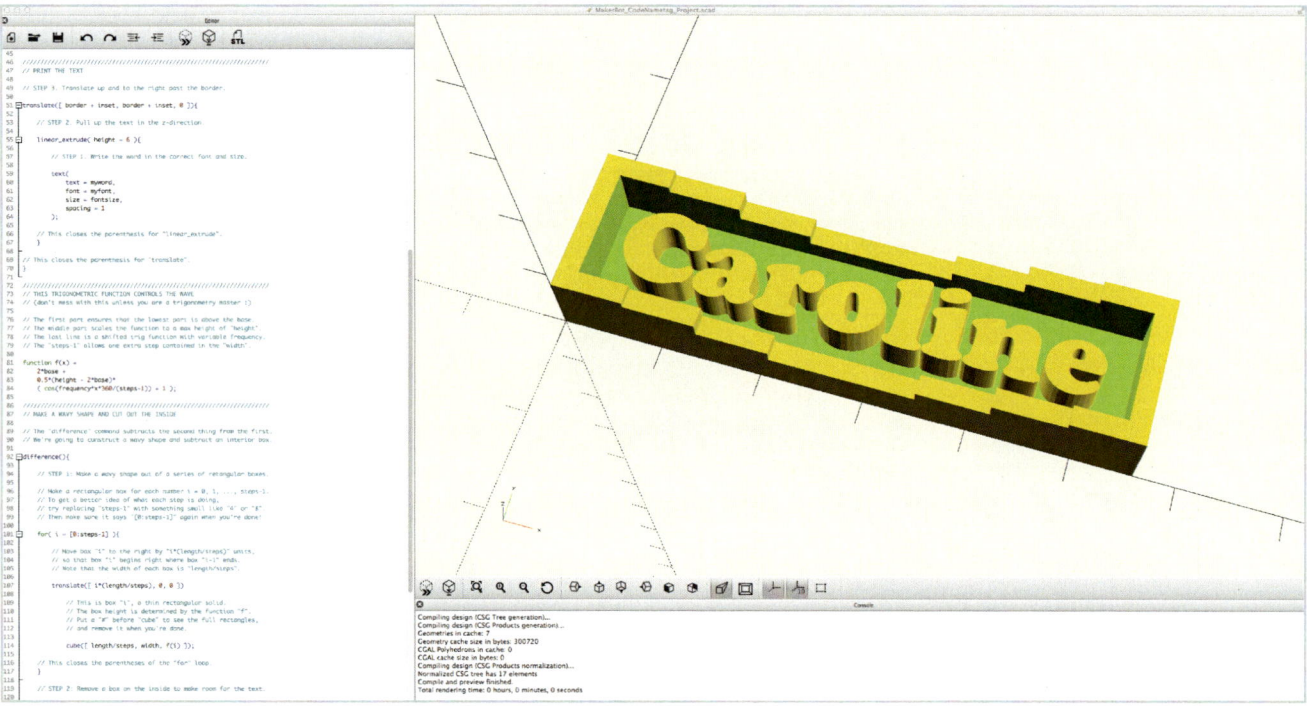

Discussion
- In groups, discuss the code among yourselves, sharing ideas about what each part of the code might be for.
- Each group should write down at least three ideas to share with the class.
- Discuss each group's ideas as a class, trying to decode the code together.

STEP 2: MODIFY TEXT AND FONT PARAMETERS

Near the top of the code are three sets of parameters that students can use to customize their nametag. The first set of parameters concerns the text, font, and font size of the nametag:

```
// TEXT AND FONT
myword = "Caroline";
myfont="Phosphate:style=Inline";
fontsize = 8;
```

You can choose to use your name or word in **myword**, but keep in mind that longer names and words will take longer to 3D print. The **myfont** parameter uses the font names of the fonts installed on your local system. Use the **Help / Font List** pull-down menu to obtain a list of your available fonts. You can drag and drop font names directly from this list into your OpenSCAD code or copy/paste into the code. You should not change **fontsize** unless the student chooses a particularly large or small font shape.

Remember that after each change, you must press **F5** (or **Function-F5**) or the **preview icon** to see the updated result in the **view area**. Compiling errors at this stage are usually due to lost quotation marks, missing semicolons, and incorrectly spelled font names.

STEP 3: ADJUST DIMENSIONS TO MATCH THE TEXT

The next set of parameters sets the overall size of the nametag:

```
// TOTAL DIMENSIONS
length = 56;
width = 15;
height = 8;
```

The **length** and **width** parameters will have to be adjusted depending on the size and length of your word choices in the previous step. The **height** parameter determines the height of the tallest part of the border wave. Compiling errors at this stage are usually due to lost semicolons.

STEP 4: STYLE THE WAVE OF THE NAMETAG BORDER

The final set of parameters determines the style of the wavy border around the outside of the nametag:

```
// BORDER CURVE STYLE
frequency = 1;
steps = 8;
border = 2;
inset = 2;
base = 2;
```

The wavy border's shape is determined by a trigonometric function, but you do not need to know any trigonometry to modify these parameters. The **frequency** parameter changes the number of waves. The **steps** parameter controls the number of times the wave height changes; lower values make stair-step shapes and higher values make smoother curves. You'll likely not need to change the **border**, **inset**, or **base** parameters, but feel free to explore adjusting them to see what happens.

STEP 5: CREATE A NEW PARAMETER FOR TEXT HEIGHT

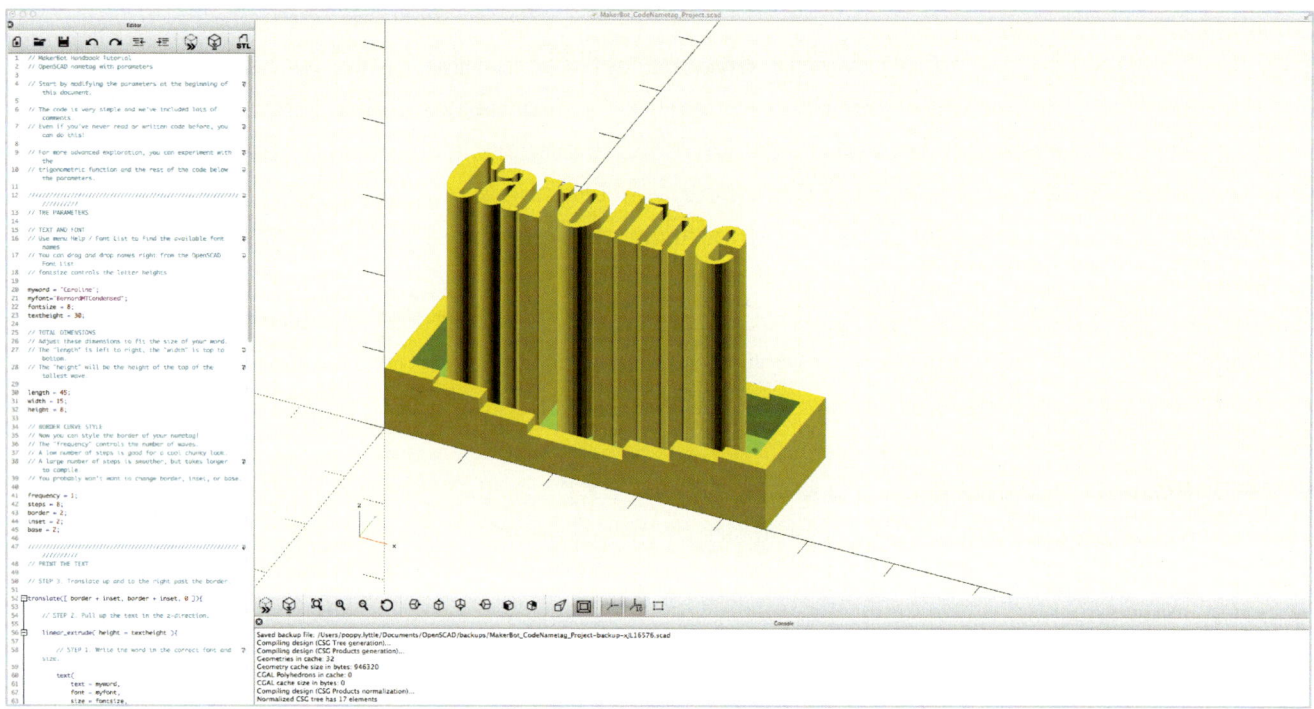

So far, you've just been modifying existing parameters in the OpenSCAD code. In this step, you'll create a new modifiable parameter. Look at the second section of the code, below the //PRINT THE TEXT comment on line 47. Notice that the code is read in reverse order: First the 2D text is created, then the letters are extruded upward, then the extruded letters are shifted up and to the right so they do not intersect the border.

- Determine the part of the code that controls the height of the letters, and figure out what to change to make the letters shorter or taller. (Hint: The text height starts out set to 6 mm.)
- Replace the numerical value on line 55 with a named parameter called **textheight**.
- Add a parameter definition to the top of the document on line 23 by typing **textheight = 6;**
- Now you can modify the text height by changing the value of this parameter on line 23.

STEP 6: CREATE A NEW PARAMETER FOR CHARACTER SPACING.
Now repeat the same process to add a new parameter called **myspacing** that controls the amount of space between the characters of the printed name.
- Try to find the place where a **myspacing** parameter would go in the code. (Hint: it's part of the **text** command and it starts out set to 1.)
- Once this parameter is set up, modify its value to adjust the character spacing to your liking. The default value of 1 represents normal spacing. Note that even small changes like modifying to 1.2 or .9 can change the spacing considerably.
- You may have to readjust the **width** of the nametag if the student makes substantial changes to the **myspacing** parameter.

STEP 7: OUTPUT AN STL MESH FOR 3D PRINTING.
Once you're done designing your nametag, export the designs to **STL** files for 3D printing:
- First, to be safe, save your OpenSCAD code file and/or write down notes about the values of the parameters you chose in your design. The exported **STL** file will not save or record those numerical values, and if there's a problem with an **STL** file, it's good to have a way to reconstruct the basic design again.
- To generate a 3D mesh suitable for printing, press **F6** (or **Function-F6**) or use the **Render** button. This process can take a lot longer than **Preview**, especially if you've chosen high values for the **step** parameter. Watch the progress bar at the bottom right of the screen.
  *Note: The **F5** action only generates a preview of the 3D object in the view area, not a complete render.*
- When the **F6** render has completed, use the pull-down menu or the **Export STL** button to export the model as an **STL** file.
- The nametag **STL** files can now be imported into **MakerBot Desktop** and 3D printed, either individually or with multiple nametags on one build plate.

CREATE: WRITE OPENSCAD CODE FROM SCRATCH TO DESIGN A MODEL

In this project, you'll write your own OpenSCAD code from scratch, making use of parameters. You can make anything you want, but it's a good idea to start with a simple design such as creating a snowman or a box and lid.

STEP 1: PLAN, THINK, AND CODE
- Before you start writing code, think about what you want to make. What parameters do you want to be able to modify in your design?
- While coding, watch out for missing semicolons, incorrect capitalization, misspellings, and parentheses that didn't get closed correctly.
- Save your work and compile with **F5** (or **Function-F5**) often. It's easier to **debug** code (fix problem sections) that has only one new line in it than it is to debug whole blocks of new code. If you compile more often, then you'll be able to target your bugs much faster.
- When approaching OpenSCAD code, it's a good idea to start by explicitly defining your parameters (**spacing = 1**). Then, if desired, go back and create variables for specific parameters that can be easily changed across your project (**spacing = myspacing; myspacing = 4**).

STEP 2: TRY NEW THINGS
- OpenSCAD has a powerful polygon() function that you might find useful in your design. For more information, see the OpenSCAD documentation about this function:
  - http://www.openscad.org/documentation.html
- In addition to linear_extrude(), there's a command called rotate_extrude() that you can use to turn 2D shapes like squares, circles, and polygons into 3D rotated objects. It works a little unexpectedly, so be ready to do some experimenting. For more information, see the OpenSCAD user manual.
- Advanced students can experiment with for() loops and if...then statements in their code, or explore how to use a module. For more information, see the OpenSCAD user manual.

STEP 3: EXPORT, PRINT, TEST, REPEAT
- When you're done designing, press **F6** (or **Function-F6**) to render your mesh model, and then **Export STL** for printing.
- Test your model. Does it work the way you want it to? Are there any parameters that you can tweak to make it better, or anything that you want to add? Remember that 3D printing is great for iterating your designs. This means that you might not get a model exactly right on the first try. Every failure is a chance to learn something and make your design better. Be willing to try, fail, and try again until you get the results you want.

FURTHER ACTIVITIES: OPENSCAD AND THINGIVERSE CUSTOMIZER

ACTIVITY 1: MODIFY OPENSCAD CODE FOR THINGIVERSE CUSTOMIZER.

Thingiverse Customizer allows users to modify parametric designs without having to interact with OpenSCAD code directly. It's relatively easy to modify a design so that it can be used in the Customizer interface; the basic idea is to add comments to your OpenSCAD code that Customizer uses to create sliders and input fields for parameters.

Materials
- Computer with OpenSCAD and downloaded code file

Steps
1. Review documentation on making a customizable thing at http://customizer.makerbot.com/docs.
2. Download code file **MakerBot_NametagCode_Project.scad** from the MakerBot Learning account on **Thingiverse**.
3. Compare with the same OpenSCAD code used in the **Thingiverse Customizer** (select **View Source** from the lower right corner of the **Customizer** at the **MakerBot Learning** account).
4. Make modifications as you explore.

ACTIVITY 2: EXPLORE THE TRIGONOMETRY USED IN THE NAMETAG.

Have precalculus students investigate the function used in the wavy border design of the nametags:

```
function f(x) =
  2*base +
  0.5*(height - 2*base)*
  ( cos(frequency*x*360/(steps-1)) + 1 );
```

In particular, what does each of the components of this function do to change the shape of the wave? Consider amplitude, frequency, and transformations. What would happen if the cosine function were replaced with the sine function? What other functions would make good nametag borders?

Materials
- Knowledge of precalculus and basic trigonometric transformations
- Computer with OpenSCAD and downloaded code file

Steps
1. Change and consider what amplitude, frequency, and transformations are doing.
2. Try changing the cosine function to sine. What happens?
3. Explore other functions that could affect the border.

ACTIVITY 3: EXPLORE RIEMANN SUMS.

The wave shape on the border of the nametag design is actually a simple **Riemann sum** approximation of the area under the graph of the function **f(x)** on an interval. Here's the code that produces the steps of the wave.

```
for( i = [0:steps-1] ){
   translate([ i*(length/steps), 0, 0 ])
      cube([ length/steps, width, f(i) ]);
```

Materials
- Knowledge of calculus and the definition of Riemann sums for definite integrals
- Computer with OpenSCAD and downloaded code file

Steps
1. Look at a small number of steps to get an idea of what is happening. What type of Riemann sum is being constructed?
2. Something subtle is happening with the steps-1 part of the function definition. Why is that part of the code here and what does it do for the design? Replace steps-1 with a value (try 4, 8, etc.) and note what happens. What does it mean about the interval being used for the Riemann sum?

KNOWLEDGE CHECKS
- What are the benefits of a parametric design?
- How do you generate basic shapes with code?
- Why is it important to use variables in OpenSCAD code?
- What are examples of parameters you might change when designing an object?
- What do you need to change or add to your OpenSCAD file to allow it to be used in Customizer?

MOVING FORWARD

Picking the right tool for your design process is an important decision. OpenSCAD really shines when you need to create designs with easily modifiable parameters. With OpenSCAD it's easy to go back and change those parameters to fit any situation you may need or make small adjustments to measurements. This flexibility allows you to iterate more on your designs. Exploring OpenSCAD further to expand upon your coding knowledge will give you the freedom to create many complex designs. Then you can take it to the next level by adding your designs to the **Thingiverse Customizer**!

PROJECT: DIGITAL SCULPTING WITH SCULPTRIS

MAKING 3D PRINTED FOSSILS

BACKGROUND

In this project, you and your students will learn how to use a free program called Sculptris. Sculptris is a digital sculpting tool that uses brush tools to manipulate a digital ball of clay, useful for creating organic shapes. The following section outlines how to incorporate Sculptris into a geological timescale and fossil unit. We'll learn how to design several complex shapes reminiscent of fossils. We'll also explore how to set up and print models that have curved surfaces. Even if you don't have a fossil unit in your class, Sculptris is a good program for any other project that requires organic shapes.

SCOPE

Students will study the timeline of life's evolution and create creatures that lived in the eras that make up the timeline. Together in groups, students will research an assigned period and create a creature that lived then. Once the creature is made, students will select which part they want to model as a fossil and print. To conclude the project, students can share their fossils, date them, and explain what the animal might have looked like and why.

PROJECT OUTLINE

Investigate: Fossils and the Geological Timescale
Explore: Designing with Sculptris
Create: Design a Shell Fossil
Create: Design a Tooth Fossil
Create: Design Your Own Fossils
Further Activities: Plaster Molds, Timescale Fossil Dig

LOGISTICS

It is recommended that students work independently on the Investigate portion of the project, and in groups during the Create portions.
- Materials
  - Fossils (real or 3D printed)
  - Computers with Sculptris and MakerBot Desktop installed
    - Download Sculptris from http://pixologic.com/sculptris/
- Technology
  - MakerBot Replicator
    - Suggested print time: 1 hour per fossil

- Computers with Sculptris and MakerBot Desktop installed
  - Download Sculptris from http://pixologic.com/sculptris/
- Three-button mouse or digital drawing tablet

Materials for Further Activities (Optional)
- Pourable plaster
- Vaseline
- Sand
- Clay
- Paper plates
- Casserole dish
- Rock cleaning tools

LEARNING OBJECTIVES
General
- Geological timescale (eon > era > period > epoch)
- Biological adaptation
- How fossils are made
- Paleontologists' work

3D Design (Digital Sculpting)
- Navigation
- Brushes — Grab, Draw, Flatten, Smooth, Crease
- How to make organic shapes
- Designing from a reference image

3D Printing
- Printing organic shapes
- Supports and rafts

TERMINOLOGY
- **Digital sculpting:** Process of creating organic shapes using brush tools, simulating clay sculpting
- **Mesh:** The collection of vertices, edges, and faces that define the shape of a 3D model; displayed in Sculptris by number of triangles
- **Polygons:** 2D surfaces the make up the **mesh**. In Sculptris, all polygons are in the shape of triangles.
- **Wireframe:** Visualization of the **mesh** of an object
- **Non-manifold:** A **mesh** that's not complete or sealed, with polygons missing or intersecting

INVESTIGATE: FOSSILS AND THE GEOLOGICAL TIMESCALE

We encourage you to explore the pacing of this project. It can be taught over multiple days or condensed into one class period.

STUDENTS WILL STUDY THE GEOLOGICAL TIMESCALE.
- Talk about the geological timeline. What makes it up? What is it used for? Break the timeline out into eons, eras, periods, and epochs.

HAVE STUDENT TEAMS EACH RESEARCH A PERIOD FROM THE PALEOZOIC, MESOZOIC, OR CENOZOIC ERA.
- What did the environment look like and how did it relate to the animals?
- What are some defining aspects of this period? What are the defining aspects of the era it falls into?
- Have the teams share their discoveries with the rest of the class.

INTRODUCE WHAT FOSSILS ARE AND HOW THEY FORM.
- Explain that fossils form from hard parts of an animal's body, and are able to form when those parts are undisturbed long enough to become covered in sediments.
- Pass around fossils to students, and prompt them to draw and label them.
- **Discussion**: Have students try to figure out where each fossil came from (animal, time period, etc).

HAVE STUDENT GROUP'S CREATE A CREATURE THAT COULD LIVE IN THE RESEARCHED PERIODS.
- Distribute large pieces of paper for them to draw out the creature, color it in, and explain each part that makes the animal special or adapted to its environment.
- Every part of the drawn creature will need to be explained. Why does the creature have a long tail? Why is it a bug?
- Have students choose a part of their animal to sculpt and print as a fossil. We recommend having students choose a small component of an animal rather than the entire animal.
- **Discussion**: Which parts of animals are likely to become fossils?

EXPLORE: DESIGNING WITH SCULPTRIS

When you open Sculptris, you'll see an image displayed. Experiment with each brush and tool to become familiar with how they function.

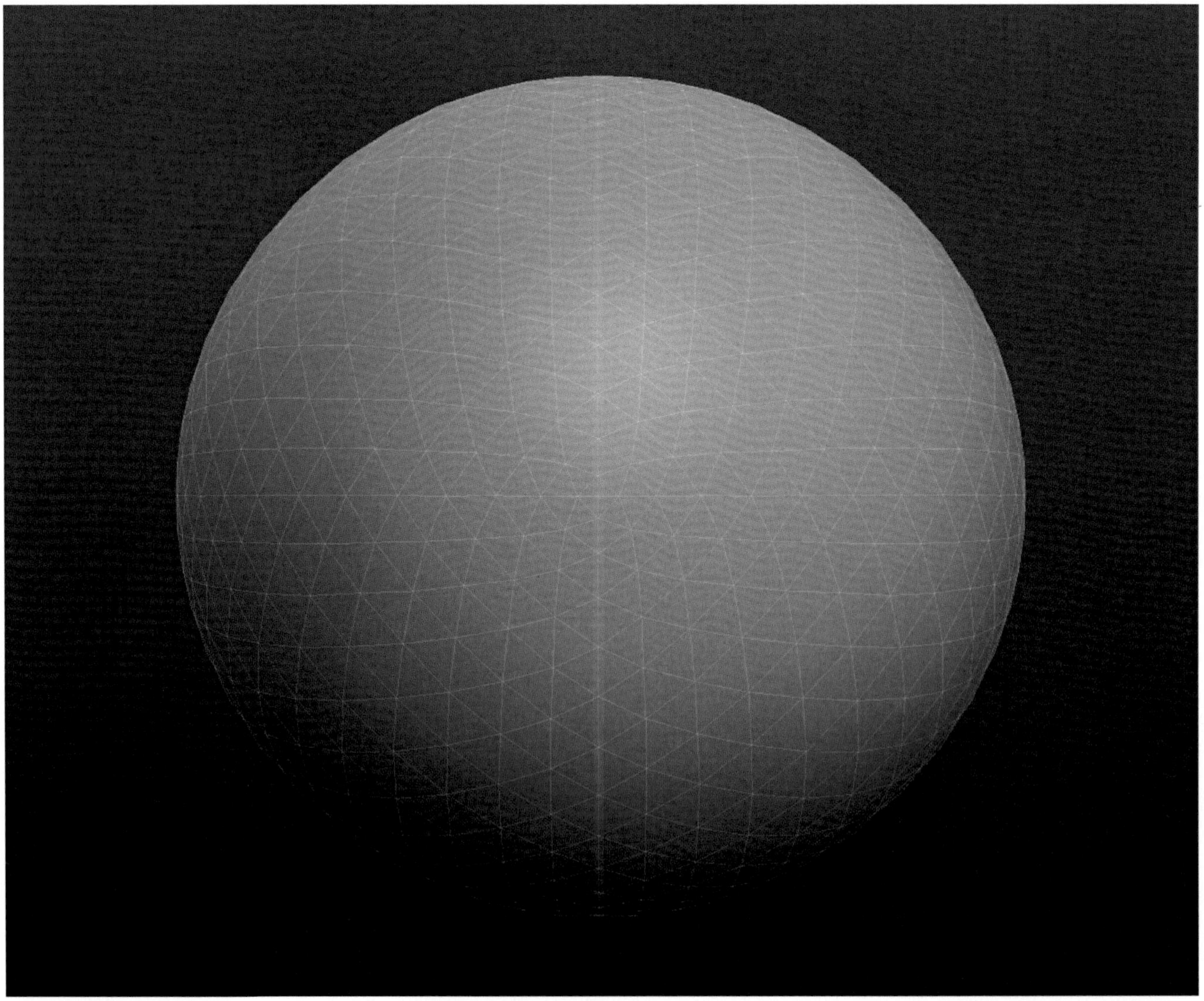

INTERFACE
1. **Digital Sphere** – A starting point for your designs
2. **Save buttons** – **Import**, **Export**, and **Save** models using these buttons
3. **Brushes** – Tools that allow you to edit your sphere (digital clay) in different ways
4. **Brush Options** – Change the size and strength of sculpting brushes
5. **Options** – Change system options and import a background image
6. **Polygon or triangle count** – Total number of triangles that define the shape of your object
7. **View Angle** – Labels each of the major views (front, left, right, etc.)
8. **Help** – Documentation shown to assist with basic hotkeys

STEP 1: LEARN HOW TO NAVIGATE.
- **Orbit** – *Right-click and drag* to orbit around the model.
- **Pan** – *Hold Alt, click and drag* with the mouse wheel.
- **Zoom** – *Scroll the mouse wheel* up and down

TIP: WHILE ORBITING, CLICK SHIFT TO SNAP TO A SPECIFIC VIEW SUCH AS TOP OR SIDE.

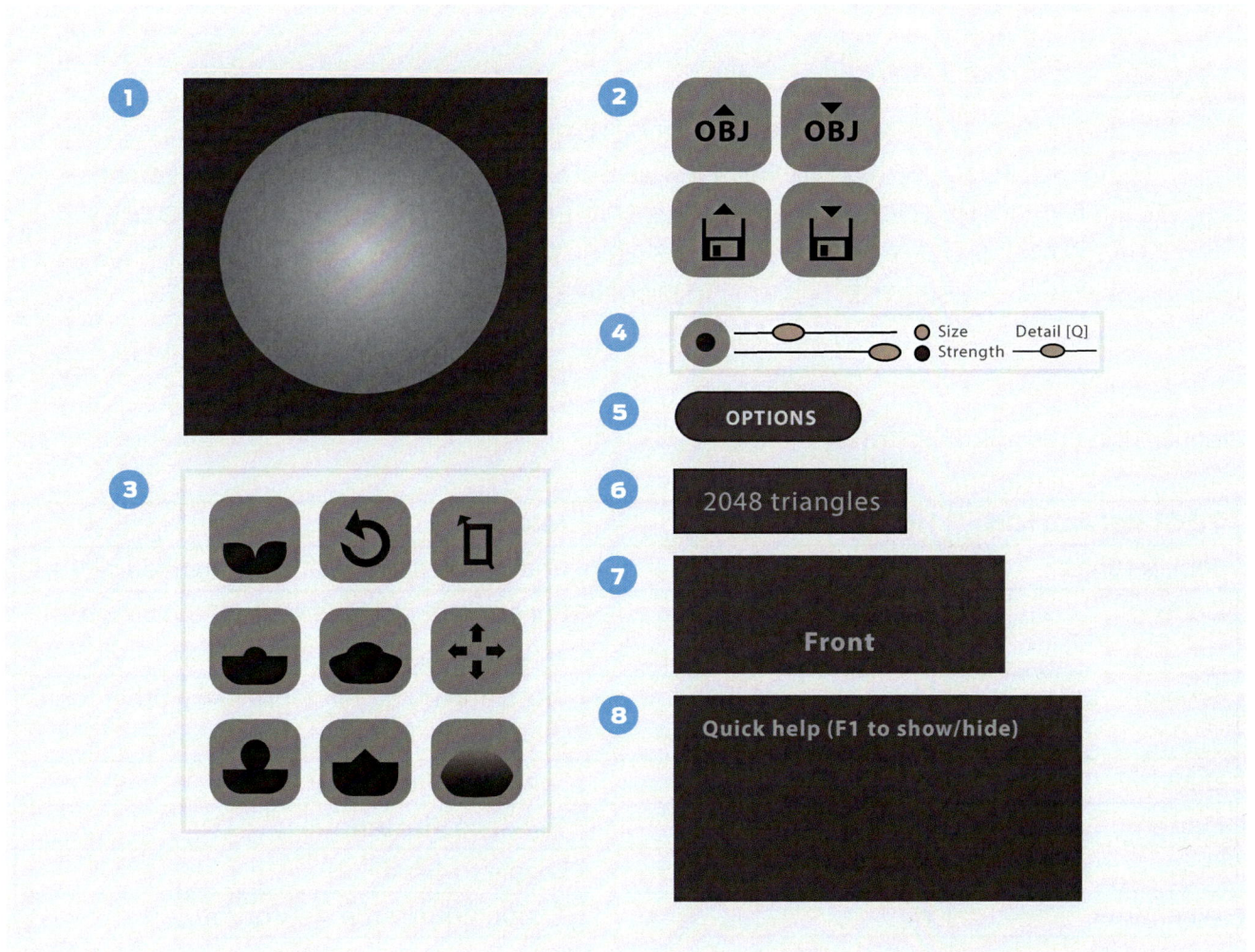

> TIP: WE FIND SCULPTRIS IS BEST USED WITH EITHER A THREE-BUTTON MOUSE OR A DIGITAL DRAWING TABLET. A LAPTOP TOUCHPAD IS NOT IDEAL FOR USING SCULPTRIS.

STEP 2: EXPERIMENT WITH THE BRUSHES.
- Explore each of the **nine brushes** in the upper left. What do you think each one will do? For example click on **Draw** and then click on the sphere to modify it. What does each brush do? Is it what you expected?
- Notice the **symmetry line** down the center of the sphere; everything you draw on one side will be mirrored onto the other. You can turn the symmetry line off with the **Symmetry** button. *Note: Designers often start modeling an object with symmetry on and then turn off for asymmetrical detail and polish.*
- For each **brush**, you can change **Size** and **Strength** from the **Brush Options** at the top of the screen. Experiment with different settings to see what they do. What do **Size** and **Strength** affect? What about **Materials**?

> TIP: YOU CAN ALSO CHANGE **BRUSH OPTIONS** WITHOUT HAVING TO MOVE YOUR MOUSE TO THE TOP OF THE SCREEN, BY PRESSING THE **SPACEBAR** TO ACTIVATE THE **TOOL SETTINGS**. THE SPACEBAR IS ONE EXAMPLE OF A **HOTKEY** THAT YOU CAN USE TO CHANGE TOOLS OR SETTINGS QUICKLY WHILE SCULPTING. SEE THE CHART FOR MORE ESSENTIAL **HOTKEYS**.

Practice using the following hotkeys:

TOOL OR ACTION	HOTKEY	NOTES
Tool Settings	Spacebar	Changes brush size and strength quickly.
Undo	Command-Z (Mac) or Control-Z (PC)	For going back a few steps in the history of your sculpt.
Smooth	Shift	Press and hold Shift while using other tools to temporarily change to **Smooth**.
Draw	D	Toggle to **Draw**.
Flatten	F	Toggle to **Flatten**.
Grab	G	Toggle to **Grab**.
Wireframe	W	Toggle **Wireframe** view on/off

STEP 3: OPTIMIZING YOUR MESH FOR 3D PRINTING
- When sculpting your model, you want to avoid **tearing** the mesh. Switch to **Wireframe** view and look at your model. What does the mesh look like? A **mesh** is basically the geometric shapes that make up your model. It's a net that should evenly cover your design without getting tangled.
- While sculpting, it's possible to tangle the mesh and create places that cannot be 3D printed. This is called making a model **non-manifold**. It can be tricky to fix and might require a different design program to resolve, so you should try to avoid sculpting actions that make the wireframe tear or intersect itself.
    - Look around your model. Is your mesh torn or intersecting itself anywhere? Within Sculptris, you might be able to fix tangled/torn meshes with the **Reduce Brush**. Select this brush, increase its **Strength**, and do several passes over the portion of the mesh in question. Try this tool out somewhere on your model.
- If your model has too many triangles, then it will take a very long time for MakerBot Desktop to **slice**. Notice the **triangle count** in the bottom left of the Sculptris screen. As a rule of thumb, you want this count to be below 100,000, which means that the resulting output file of your model should be below 10 MB, and easy to slice for 3D printing. Keeping the triangle count low also helps the program run smoother.
    - To reduce triangle count, use **Reduce** or **Reduce Selected**. Notice the effect these tools have on the **triangle count** at the bottom left of your screen.

STEP 4: RESET YOUR WORKSPACE AND CONFIGURE THE TOOLS AND BRUSHES.
Now that you've experimented with different settings, it's important to start with a fresh canvas and brushes. Follow these steps to set up your workspace for the next section.
- To start over again with a fresh sphere to work with, click on the **Sphere** button and then select **New Scene**.
- Make sure that **Symmetry** is activated. A **symmetry line** will be visible on your sphere.
- Activate or deactivate the **Wireframe** button, depending upon your preference.
- Make sure **Airbrush** is turned on.
- Configure your brush size and strength settings. You can always change these later as you sculpt, but a good place to start is with:
    - **Grab: Strength** in the center, **Detail** in the center; turn off **Global**.
    - **Draw: Strength** in the center, **Detail** on the right; turn on **Clay** and then turn on **Soft**.
    - **Smooth: Strength** in the center, **Detail** in the center.
    - **Flatten: Strength** in the center, **Detail** in the center.

CREATE: DESIGN A SHELL FOSSIL

In this section, you'll use Sculptris to create a shell fossil. Some fossils of this shape come from ammonites, mollusks that started to appear about 240 million years ago. They're one of the most abundant fossils found today. The ammonite is extinct now, but looks very similar to the nautilus, which is living today.

We'll go through the design steps one at a time, so don't worry if you're just a beginner.

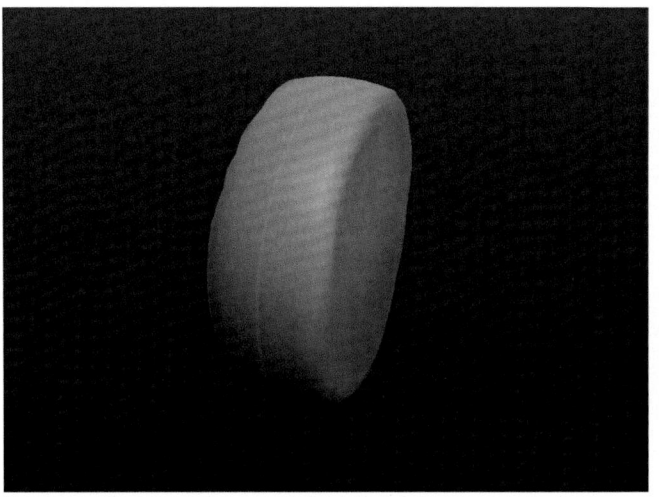
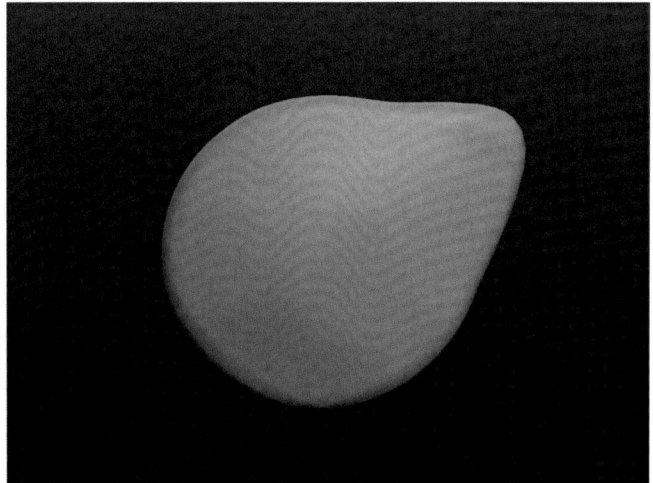

STEP 1: FLATTEN INTO A HOCKEY PUCK SHAPE.

Your first goal is to make a flat cylindrical shape.
- Press **New Sphere** and then **New Scene** to start with a fresh sphere.
- **Right-click to orbit** around the sphere so that the **symmetry line** is not visible, ensuring you're working on one side of the model only. Now everything you do on the front of the sphere will be mirrored on the back.
- Choose **Flatten** and set it to maximum **Size** using either the **Brush Options** or **Tool Settings**.
- Flatten the sphere by drawing on it with **Flatten** until it looks like a hockey puck. Orbit around the object to make sure it has the correct shape.

STEP 2: ELONGATE ONE SIDE OF YOUR OBJECT.

Pull out one side of the shape to make a place for the helix in the next step. The goal is to get something that looks like the above image.
- Choose the **Grab** brush and make the brush size fairly large.
- Pull out one side of the object.
- Orbit around to make sure that your grab didn't leave a dent along the symmetry line. If it did, then use **Draw** to fill it in (or **Undo** and try again).

TIP: REMEMBER THAT YOU CAN ACCESS **SMOOTH** QUICKLY BY **PRESSING SHIFT**.

STEP 3: DRAW A HELIX SHAPE.

Now you'll start from the tab you made in the previous step and draw a spiral inward to the center of the object.
- Select **Draw** and change the **Size**.
- Use your mouse to draw a spiral starting from the tab and ending in the center.
- You can use **Crease** to emphasize the indents of the helix, or **Smooth** to de-emphasize those indents.

STEP 4: DRAW DETAIL LINES AROUND THE HELIX.

Your goal in this step is to continue refining your fossil by adding smaller details.

- Select **Draw** and decrease the brush size.
- Draw details on the helix (see pictures for inspiration)
- Orbit around and make sure that your outside lines connect to the other side of the object. Use **Draw** to extend your lines to the symmetry line if necessary.

TIP: BECAUSE SCULPTRIS'S DEFAULT UNITS IS INCHES, THE MODEL ITSELF WILL BE VERY SMALL WHEN IMPORTED INTO MAKERBOT DESKTOP. WHEN IMPORTED, YOU SHOULD BE PROMPTED TO RESCALE. IF NOT, OPEN **SCALE** AND PRESS **IN » MM**.

STEP 5: FINISHING TOUCHES

Experiment with more brushes and settings to modify and polish the shape of your model:

- Use **Grab** to make the overall model thinner or thicker. First, zoom out and select the largest possible brush size. Then grab the fossil from the front face and push in or out to change its width.
- Soften rough sections by orbiting around and smoothing.
- Make the design your own!

STEP 6: SAVE, EXPORT, AND PRINT YOUR FOSSIL

- **Save** your design to the computer so you can modify it later.
- **Export** an **OBJ** of your completed model to your computer. The export feature uses OBJ files automatically.
- Within **Prepare** in MakerBot Desktop, choose **Add File** and load your design. If a window pops up asking if you want to scale your object, choose **Rescale Object** when prompted.
- You'll likely need to print with **Supports** due to the organic shape of your model. Try to reorient and angle your model on the build platform so your fossil can print with minimal supports.

CREATE:
DESIGN A TOOTH FOSSIL

In this section, you'll use Sculptris to model a fossil of an herbivore's teeth. Herbivores often have several pairs of wide, ridged molars used to grind leaves and other food. By discovering fossils like this, archeologists can learn a lot about the animal's diet and eating habits. What story will your fossil tell?

In this walkthrough, we'll assume that you've already completed the shell fossil and understand how to use the basic tools, settings, brushes, and hotkeys in Sculptris.

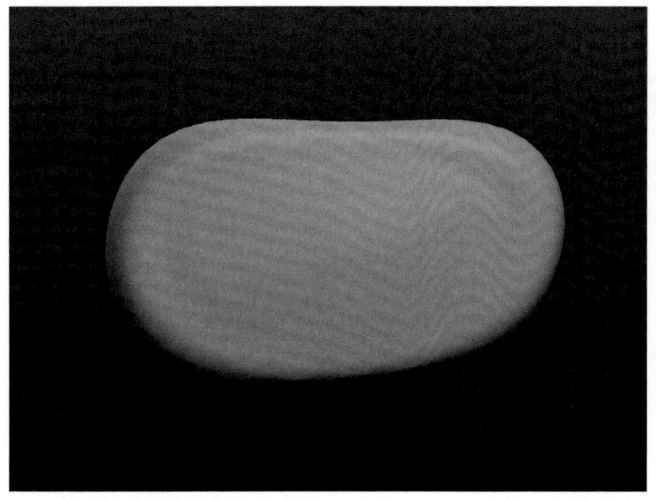
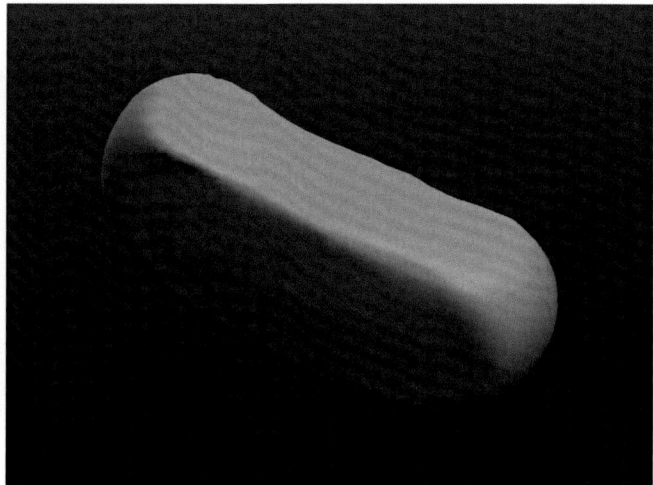

STEP 1: FORM THE BASIC STARTING SHAPE FOR YOUR OBJECT.

To begin sculpting the herbivore teeth, create an oblong shape. You'll form and carve teeth from this block.

- Use **New Sphere** to start a new file. Make sure **Symmetry** is turned on.
- Orbit around so that the **symmetry line** is hidden and use **Flatten** to shape the sphere.
- Use **Grab** with a large brush size to pull part of the model to the side. Orbit around to make sure that things look clean along the symmetry line.

STEP 2: FLATTEN ALONG THE SYMMETRY LINE.

Herbivores have flat molars, so in the next step flatten out the top of the shape. This is where you'll sculpt the biting surfaces of the teeth. Make sure that the flattened surface has the symmetry line running through it.

- Orbit around so that you can see the **symmetry line**.
- **Flatten** the shape along the symmetry line. Use **Reduce** or **Smooth** if you see your mesh tearing.

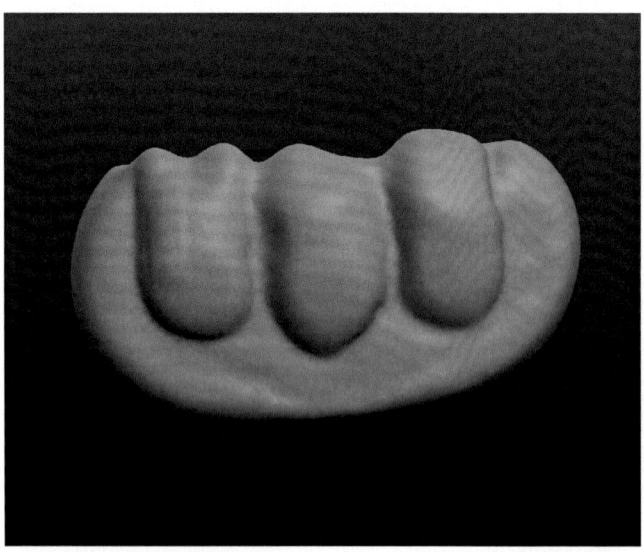

STEP 3: DRAW THE SIDE SURFACES OF THE TEETH.

Think about what molars look like from the side. Our next step is to sculpt the shape of three herbivore teeth. Everyone's model will look different, but in this step you're aiming for something like the image to the left.

- Orbit to one side of the model.
- Use **Draw** and **Crease** to sculpt the side shapes of three molars. Remember to change the **Size** and **Strength** of your brushes as needed.
- **Grab** onto one or two points on each molar. Change the size of your brush to add variety.

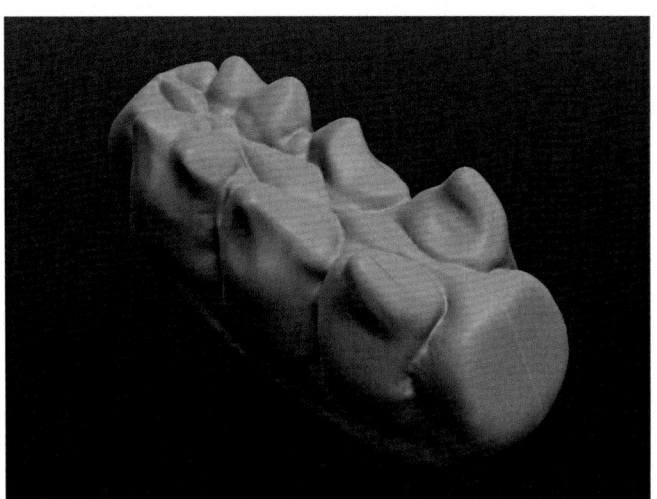

STEP 4: CREASE THE TOP OF THE TEETH.
Look up a few pictures of teeth from different herbivores that live today. Use these pictures for reference during the next steps.
- Use **Crease** to indent between the molars and down the center. **Orbit** around often to see how things look from each angle.
- Use **Grab** to pull on certain points of the teeth.

STEP 5: ADD FINISHING TOUCHES
- If your fossil seems too wide or too thin, then zoom out and use **Grab** at its largest brush size to make the entire model thinner or wider. Make sure you orbit to look at the model from all angles.
- Put finishing touches on your model, using **Smooth** to iron out rough spots and other brushes to make adjustments.
- **Flatten** the bottom section to help with printing.

STEP 6: SAVE, EXPORT, AND PRINT YOUR DESIGN
- **Save** your Sculptris file and **Export** your model as an **OBJ**.
- Repeat steps from the shell fossil model to prepare and print your model.

CREATE: DESIGN YOUR OWN FOSSILS

Now use the sculpting techniques from the previous sections to design and print your own Sculptris files. Refer back to the Investigate section for ideas on types of custom creature fossils to create. Once you've completed your design, **Save**, **Export**, and **Print** your fossil model.

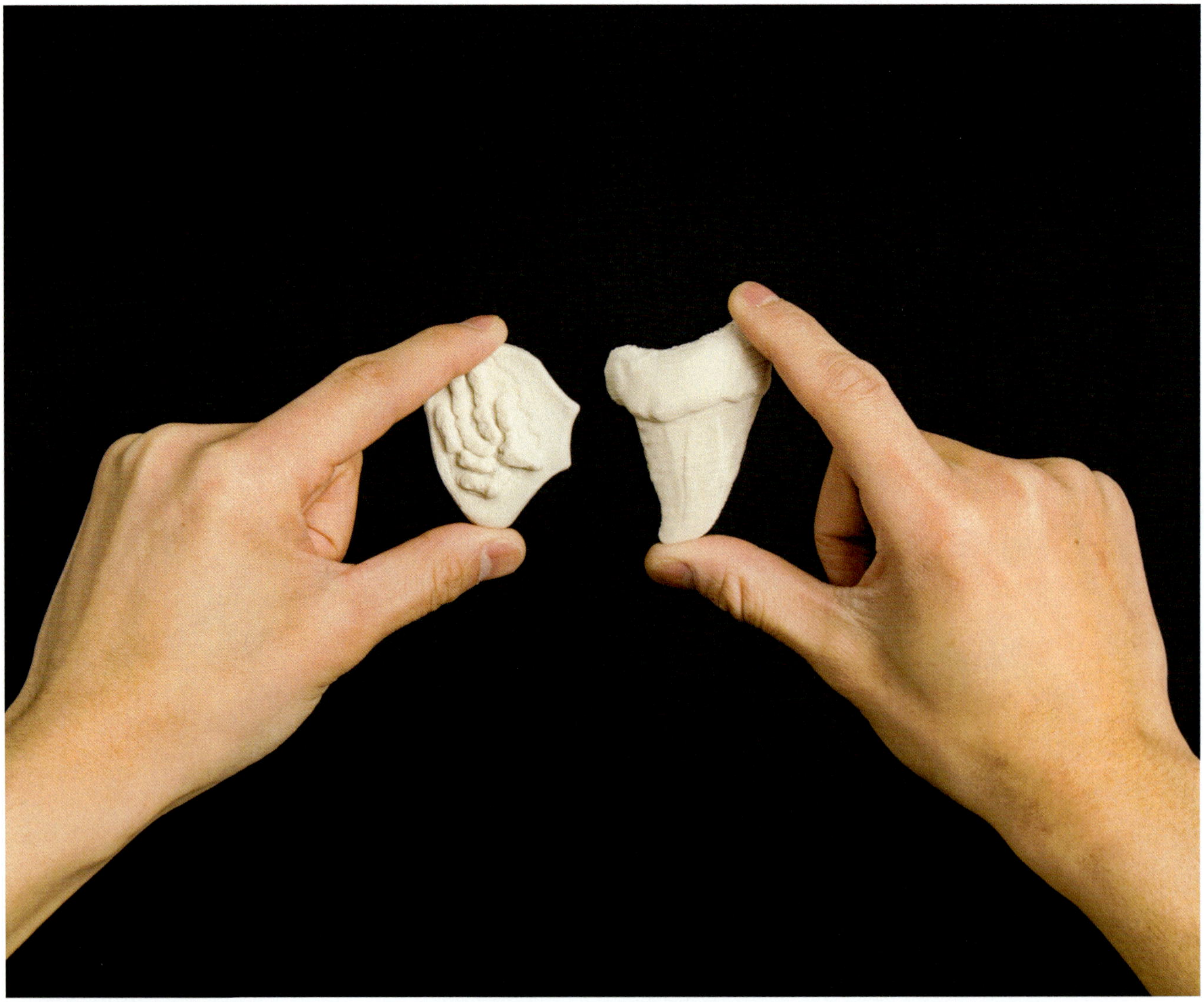

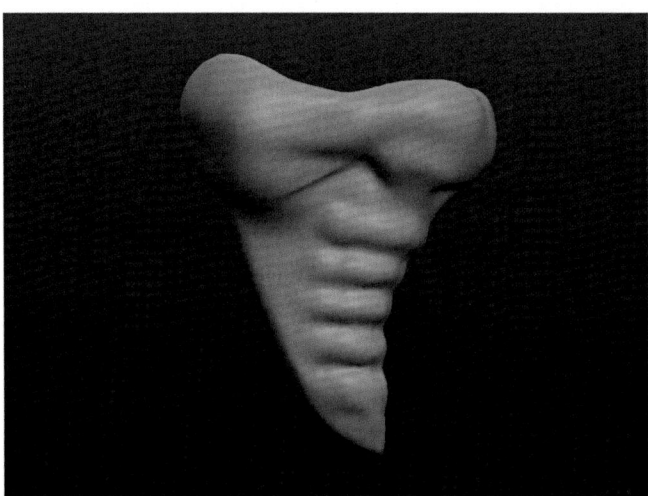

For More Inspiration
Check out these two designs made using the same set of tools.

Here's a model of a fossilized carnivore tooth. How is this carnivore tooth different from the herbivore teeth we made earlier, and why? What does the shape of the tooth say about the eating behavior of the animal?

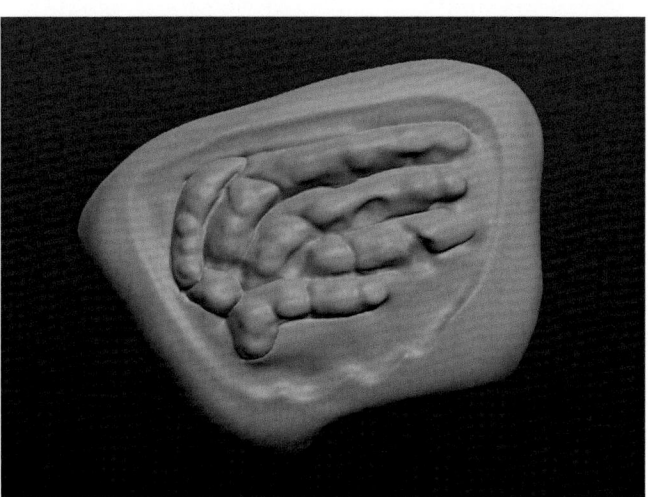

Here's a model of fossilized fin bones. Why do you think only the bones of the fin remain? What does the shape of the fossilized bones say about the shape of the fin they came from?

FURTHER ACTIVITIES: PLASTER MOLDS, TIMESCALE FOSSIL DIG

ACTIVITY 1: CREATE PLASTER FOSSILS FROM MOLDS.

Fossils form in seven ways: carbon films, coal, mineral replacement, molds or casts, original remains, trace fossils, and tracks or burrows.

After the Create projects have been completed, learn more about the different ways that fossils form in nature, by making a plaster mold of your own fossil.

Materials
- Pourable plaster (Plaster of Paris)
- Vaseline or mold release
- Clay
- Paper plates

Steps
1. Make a disk of clay on each plate, and have the students press their fossils into the clay.
2. Apply vaseline into the fossil cavity.
3. Pour Plaster of Paris into the cavity and leave overnight.
4. The next day, have the students remove their plaster fossils from the clay and share the animals they've made. Review or finish covering the seven ways that fossilization occurs in nature.
5. Have the students swap their fossils with classmates. Prompt them to sketch the fossils and try to figure out what kind of animal it was and why it looks the way it does.

ACTIVITY 2: PALEONTOLOGIST DIG — BURY AND UNEARTH FOSSILS

Demonstrate how paleontologists work at a dig site in this mock fossil dig. Student groups will share their projects with the class in the creative activity outlined below.

Materials
- Sand
- Casserole dishes
- Rock cleaning tools

Steps
1. Have your students design a creature from the beginning of the Paleolithic Era and evolve it through the Mesozoic Era.
2. Each student can sculpt and print a series of small fossils that represent what the animal might have been like in each era.
3. After printing, each student can assemble a soil timeline in a disposable casserole tray, by burying the fossils in sand in the order that reflects the Precambrian ages (oldest is deepest, and so on).
4. Have the students swap trays and learn how to properly uncover and date fossils in the same way paleontologists do.
5. The students should date the fossils based on where they were found and what kind of creature they likely represent.

TIP: DUE TO THE NUMBER OF FOSSILS REQUIRED, PRINT EACH MODEL AT A SMALLER SIZE TO SAVE PRINTING TIME.

KNOWLEDGE CHECKS
- How is digital sculpting different from other modeling tools?
- What are the strengths and weaknesses of Sculptris?
- How do you use Symmetry?
- How do you navigate in Sculptris?
- What are good tricks for successfully printing organic shapes?
- How do you use supports and rafts in MakerBot Desktop?
- Why do you need to scale Sculptris objects in MakerBot Desktop?

MOVING FORWARD
Digital sculpting can be a very powerful tool for creating organic shapes. Research professional designers using digital sculpting programs to get a glimpse of the amazing things that can be made with enough practice.

PROJECT: SOLID MODELING WITH 123D DESIGN

EXPERIMENTAL ENGINEERING: BUILD A BRIDGE

BACKGROUND
In this project, you and your students will learn how to use a free program called 123D Design. 123D Design is a solid modeling tool that uses basic shapes and sketches to build objects. It's useful for any project that requires specific dimensions and/or multiple interlocking parts. The following sections outline how you can incorporate 123D Design into engineering, physics, and specifically bridge building units. We'll learn how to design 3D printed connectors that can be used to assemble a bridge structure. We'll also explore how 3D printing can affect the structural strength and integrity of your models.

SCOPE
Students will design and build a scale model of a bridge using only balsa wood, 3D printed connectors, and glue. In the Investigate portion of the project, students will research various bridge designs and begin brainstorming their own. Then, in the Explore and Create sections, they'll learn how to use 123D Design to model different types of connectors for their bridge. Finally, they'll assemble and test their bridge for structural integrity. In Further Activities, they can take this project to the next level by building and testing other structures using a similar process.

PROJECT OUTLINE
Investigate: Bridges and Other Load-Bearing Structures
Explore: Modeling with 123D Design
Create: Modeling Strength Test Beams
Create: Design a Four-Point Connector
Create: Design a Hexagonal Connector
Create: Design an Arc Connector
Create: Design Additional Connectors
Further Activities: Bridge Testing, Upcycled Structures

LOGISTICS

It's recommended that students work independently on the Investigate portion of the project, and in groups during the Create portions. You'll need access to a large area during the bridge assembly portion of the project.

- Technology
  - Computers with 123D Design and MakerBot Desktop installed (http://www.123dapp.com/design)
  - MakerBot Replicator
    - Suggested print time: 30 minutes – 90 minutes per part
- Materials
  - Balsa wood strips (1/8 x 1/8 in) or something similar (toothpicks or popsicle sticks can also work)
  - Wood glue
  - Graph paper
  - Weights (brass weight set, bricks, etc.)

LEARNING OBJECTIVES

General
- Understand bridge structures
- Identify the similarities and differences between various bridge designs
- Define trusses and their importance
- Explore how different geometric shapes handle force
- Consider the economics of building objects with material and price limitations

3D Printing
- When to take advantage of 3D printing versus using existing materials
- Overhangs and bridging
- Impact of print settings on model strength and material use
- Importance of infill, shells, and print orientation

3D Design (Solid Modeling)
- Sketching
- Extruding
- Designing with tolerance

TERMINOLOGY

- **Extrude:** Tool used to turn a 2D shape into a 3D object
- **Perspective View:** Adjusts the point of view to match how the human eye sees. Objects that are farther away appear smaller than objects that are closer to the "camera."
- **Orthographic View:** Adjusts the point of view to a single perspective. All objects of the same size appear to be the same size, no matter their distance from the "camera."
- **Chamfer:** A flat angled cut to the edge of a component, often used as a finishing technique

INVESTIGATE: BRIDGES AND OTHER LOAD-BEARING STRUCTURES

Bridges have been used for a very long time to allow transportation over difficult geographical areas. Bridge building involves a lot of very precise engineering because the structure needs to be able to withstand weight, heavy use, and environmental impacts. In this section, students will research different types of bridges to find out the strengths and weaknesses of each, as well as explore how bridge design has evolved through time.

Have your students research existing bridges in use today. **Explore** the following types of bridges. Prompt the class to explain the strengths and weaknesses of each:
- Arch bridge
- Beam bridge
- Truss bridge
- Suspension bridge

Find a non-bridge structure that incorporates similar designs to one (or more) of the bridges your class has researched. For example, the Eiffel Tower in Paris, France.

Once the students have researched and compared bridge designs, have them research the **Tacoma Narrows Bridge** to see an example of a bridge design gone wrong.

Before venturing into the **Create** sections, prompt your students with the following:
- You've been tasked as a newly hired civil engineer to create a next-generation bridge for your community. With the assistance of 3D printing and your knowledge of 123D Design and bridge construction, you'll use balsa wood and 3D printed connector pieces to build a scale model of the bridge and test it to discover how much weight it can hold.

EXPLORE: MODELING WITH 123D DESIGN

In this exploration, you'll learn the basics of 123D Design. When you open the 123D Design software and start a new project, you'll see a window like the one below.

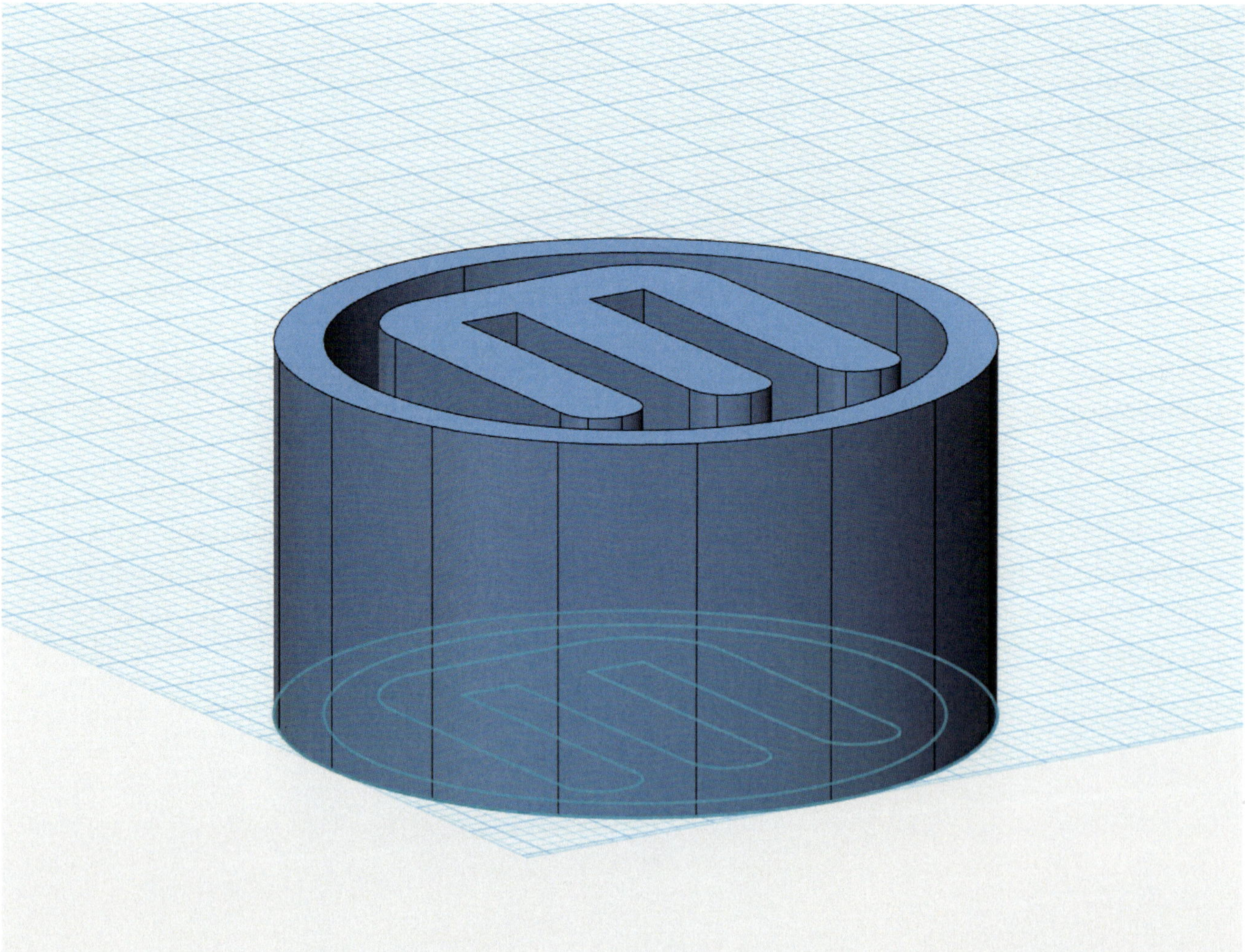

INTERFACE

1. **Workplane** – This is the default grid upon which you build your object(s). Your cursor will snap to the grid when sketching and placing primitives.
2. **Origin** – (0,0) on the Workplane. It's good practice to model your objects at the origin.
3. **123D Design menu** – Save file, export, and other system options are found here.
4. **Undo/Redo buttons** – Undo or redo recent actions.
5. **3D Modeling Toolbar** – All modeling functions are found here.
6. **View Cube** – Use to orient your view around your scene.
7. **View and Navigation Toolbar** – Use this menu to change your view and/or change the way objects appear in your scene.
8. **Advanced Primitives menu** – Premade objects available to drag into your scene for modification. *Note: some of these primitives are only available through a premium membership.*
9. **Units** – Change your default modeling units to mm, cm, or in.
10. **Snap** – Change the default snap interval when modeling objects.

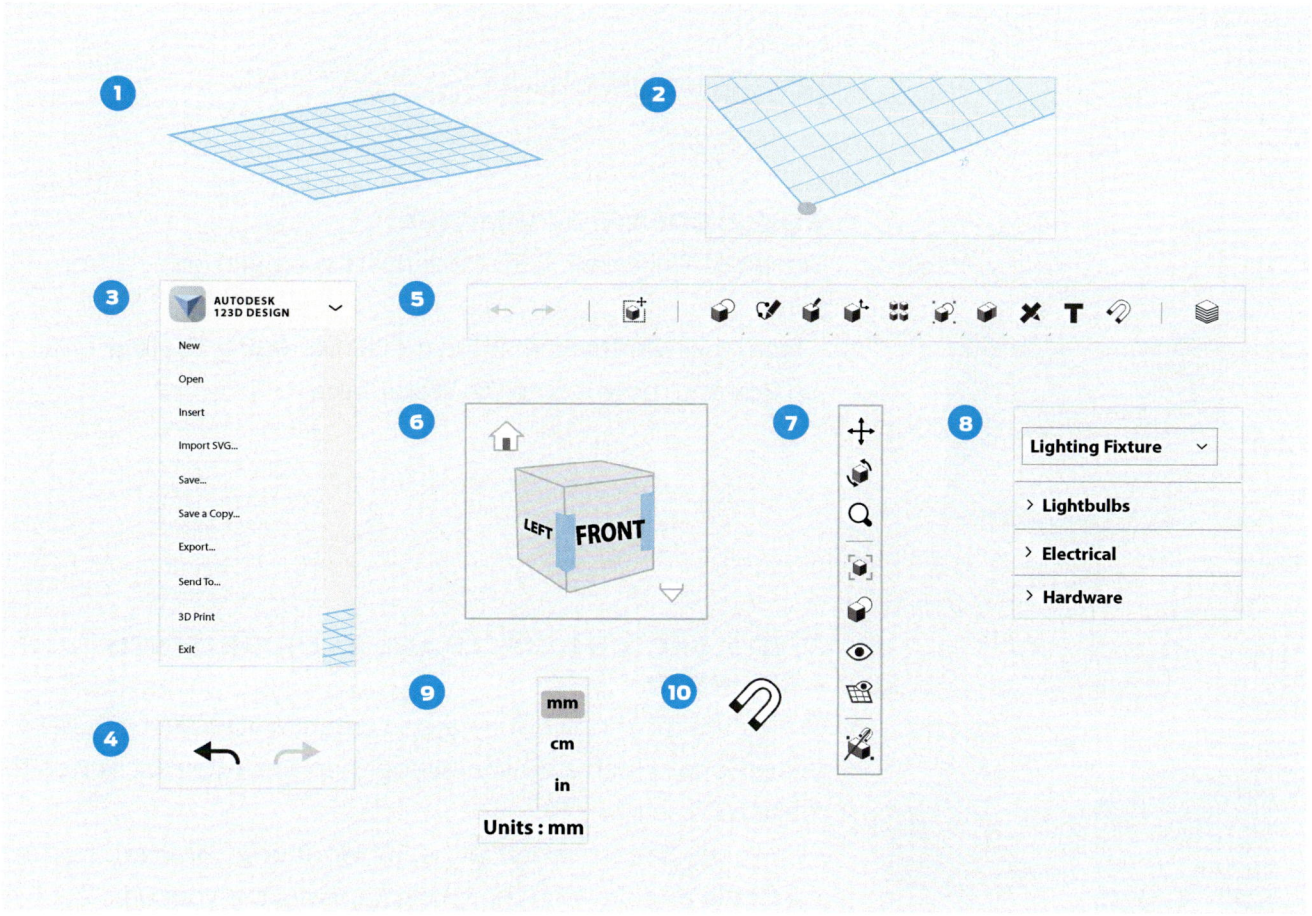

STEP 1: LEARN HOW TO NAVIGATE.
If you're going to design and build in 123D Design, then you'll need to know how to move and look around in the environment. There are three different ways that you can navigate in 123D Design:
- The **View Cube** in the top right corner of the screen allows you to orbit around your scene. Click on a side, corner, or edge of the cube to orbit the **Workplane** to that view angle, or just click and drag the View Cube to manually rotate your scene. While your mouse is over the **View Cube**, you'll also see a **home icon** (tiny house) that you can press to return to the default view, and a tiny drop down menu that you can use to change your view between **Orthographic** and **Perspective**.
- You can also navigate by using your mouse from the **Workplane** itself:
  - **Orbit** – *Right-click and drag* to orbit around and see the Workplane from different viewing angles.
  - **Pan** – *Click the center mouse wheel and drag*.
  - To **zoom** in and out, use the scroll wheel of your mouse.
  - A laptop touchpad is not ideal when using 123D Design; make sure you have a three-button mouse so you can easily use the full functionality of 123D Design.
- Finally, you can use the **pan**, **orbit**, and **zoom** buttons along the right side of your screen.

TIP: CHANGE YOUR VIEW TO ORTHOGRAPHIC.

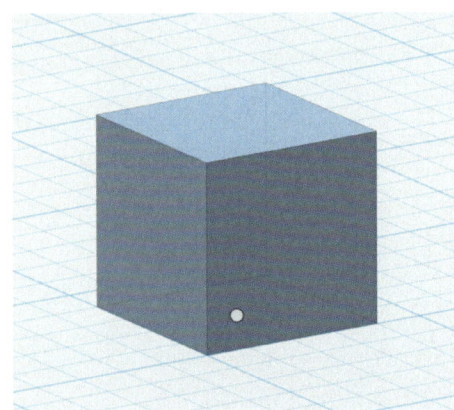

STEP 2: CREATE A PRIMITIVE.
Similar to Tinkercad, 123D Design lets you build objects from primitives.
- From the **Primitives** menu in the **3D Modeling Toolbar**, click a **Box** and move it onto the **Workplane**.

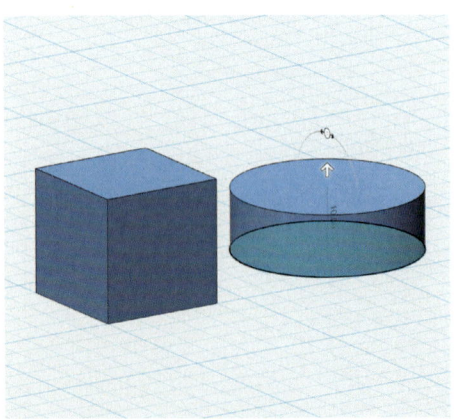

STEP 3: SKETCH A CIRCLE AND EXTRUDE IT INTO A CYLINDER.
One of the most powerful ways to create a 3D object in 123D Design is to sketch a 2D shape and then **Extrude** that sketch to make a 3D solid.
- From the **Sketch** menu in the **3D Modeling Toolbar**, choose a **Circle** and draw on the **Workplane** next to your box.
- From the **Construct** menu, choose **Extrude** and click on the light blue area of your circle sketch. You'll see an arrow appear allowing you to drag your circle upward to create a cylinder.

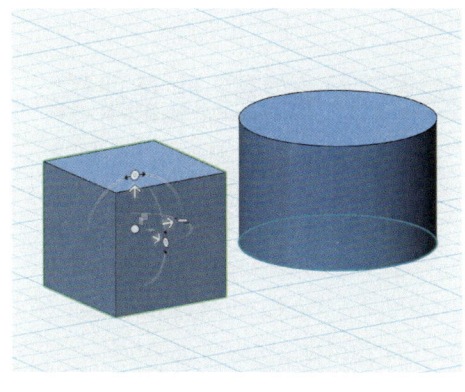

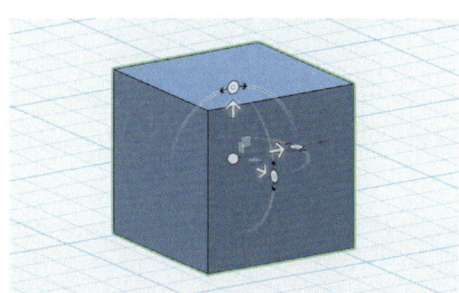

STEP 4: MOVE AND ROTATE WITH THE MOVE TOOL.

The **Move** tool is essential to moving objects in 123D Design. It allows you to reposition and rotate objects around the **Workplane**. This is also essential for learning how to reposition objects in relation to one another. Whether you're placing objects next to, on top of, or inside each other, you'll use the **Move** tool to accomplish these tasks.

- Click on your cylinder and notice the menu that appears on the bottom of your window. The first option in this menu is the **Move** tool. Click on it to initiate a move.
- The three arrows that appear allow you to move your object along the **x**, **y**, and **z axes**. The circular handles next to the arrows allow you to rotate your object along each axis.
- Use the **Move** tool to place your cylinder so it sits directly on top of the cube. **Orbit** your view to make sure it's in the correct position.

TIP: YOU CAN ALSO ACCESS THE **MOVE** TOOL FROM THE **3D MODELING TOOLBAR**. ADJUSTING YOUR VIEW WITH THE **VIEW CUBE** CAN HELP MAKE SURE YOU'RE MOVING OR ROTATING ALONG THE CORRECT AXIS. THOUGH IT'S TEMPTING, DO NOT USE THE CENTER CIRCLE TO CLICK AND DRAG YOUR OBJECT AROUND YOUR WORKPLANE. YOU'LL LOSE A SENSE OF 3D SPACE AND WHERE YOUR OBJECT IS LOCATED.

CREATE: MODELING STRENGTH TEST BEAMS

When engineers design large structures like bridges, they need to determine the appropriate size, shape, and materials to use in construction. They accomplish this by researching, testing, and analyzing a lot of different parts until they find the right mix of strength and weight.

In this section, we'll design and print several test beams to explore this concept. By experimenting with different designs, print settings, and print orientations, you'll gather key information needed to build a structurally sound bridge in the next section.

STEP 1: SKETCH A RECTANGLE.

Let's start by sketching a **3.0 x 0.25 in rectangle**.

Note: Most balsa wood strips are measured in inches, so we'll use inches as our default unit.

- In the bottom right corner of the screen, make sure that the **Units** are set to **inches (in)**.
- Near the **View Cube**, use the tiny dropdown menu to change your view from **Perspective** to **Orthographic**.
- Select **Sketch > Rectangle** from the **3D Modeling Toolbar** at the top center of the screen.
- To use **Sketch > Rectangle**, click on the grid to begin sketching. Click again to select the starting corner of your rectangle. Click a third time to pick your endpoint.
  - Use this process to sketch a rectangle that has one corner at the **origin** (lower left) and the opposite corner at the point **3.0 in** to the right and **0.25 in** up (as shown), or type in the values and confirm with **enter**. Either way, make sure your rectangle is **3.0 x 0.25 in**.

TIP: ONCE YOU'VE COMPLETED YOUR SKETCH, CLICK THE GREEN CHECKMARK TO EXIT SKETCHING MODE.

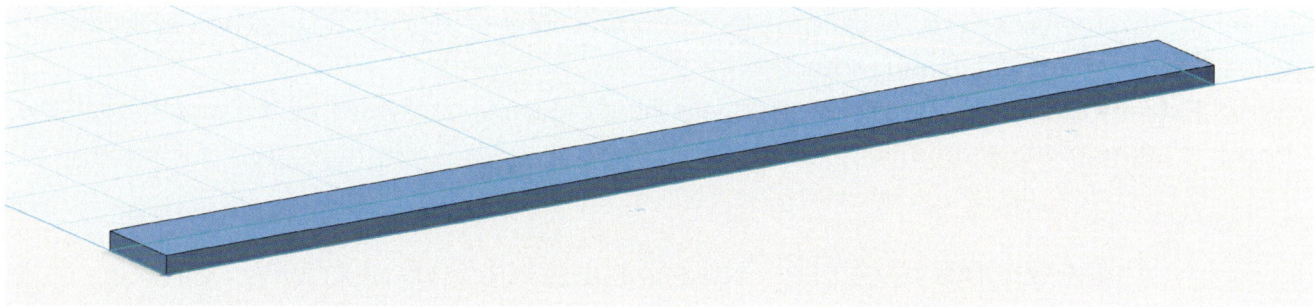

STEP 2: EXTRUDE THE SKETCH.

Now extrude your rectangle sketch to make it a 3D object. The resulting shape will be the first model for the "stress test" at the end of the lesson, so you'll need to make the 3D shape very thin: just **0.05 in**.

- Make sure that the **Snap** setting in the lower right corner of the screen is set to 0.1 in.
- Select **Construct > Extrude** from the **3D Modeling Toolbar**.
- Click on the rectangle sketch and type **0.05** into the value box. Press **Enter/Return** to confirm or click away from the object.
- From the **123D Design menu** at the upper left, select **Export STL** to save a 3D printable file of your test beam. Name the file to indicate that this is **Test Beam 1**.

TIP: IN THE **VIEW AND NAVIGATION TOOLBAR**, MOUSE OVER THE SMALL EYE ICON AND SELECT **HIDE SKETCHES**. THIS ACTION WILL HIDE YOUR ORIGINAL RECTANGLE SKETCH UNDER YOUR OBJECT.

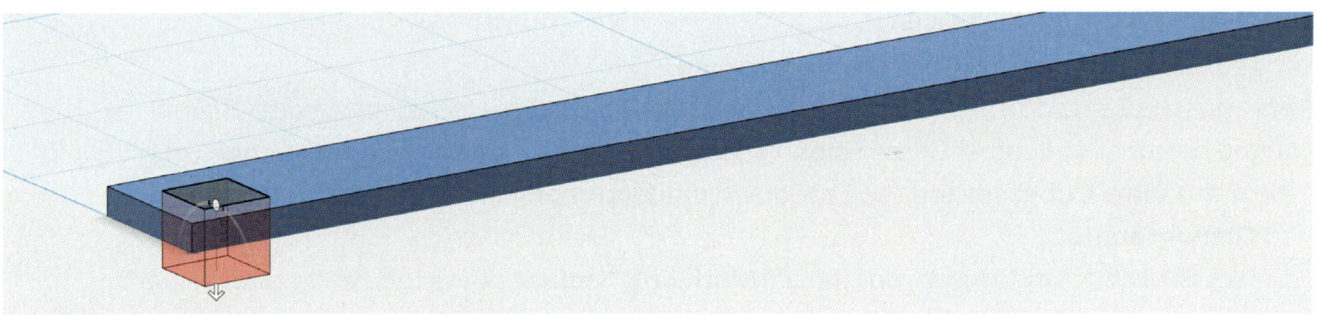

STEP 3: USE SKETCH AND EXTRUDE TO MODIFY THE TEST BEAM.

Now you'll use the same set of tools to remove material from the test beam. Maybe this will make the beam stronger, or maybe it will make it weaker; what do you think? At the end of this exploration, you'll print your test beams and find out.

- Select **Sketch > Rectangle** and click on the top face of your test beam. This will make the top of the beam the surface on which the new rectangle will be drawn. Click **Top** on the **View Cube** to get a bird's-eye view.
- Your goal is to draw a small square with **0.125 in** sides near the left side of the beam.
- To get these dimensions exactly, click to place the first corner of your rectangle. Then, enter the value **0.125** for both length and width.
- Select **Extrude** and click on the **0.125 in** square. Drag the arrow backward, all the way through the beam, to subtract material.

TIPS: USE **TAB** TO GET FROM ONE VALUE BOX TO THE NEXT WITHOUT HAVING TO CLICK. **ORBIT** AROUND YOUR MODEL TO ENSURE THAT THE HOLE WENT ALL THE WAY THROUGH THE BEAM.

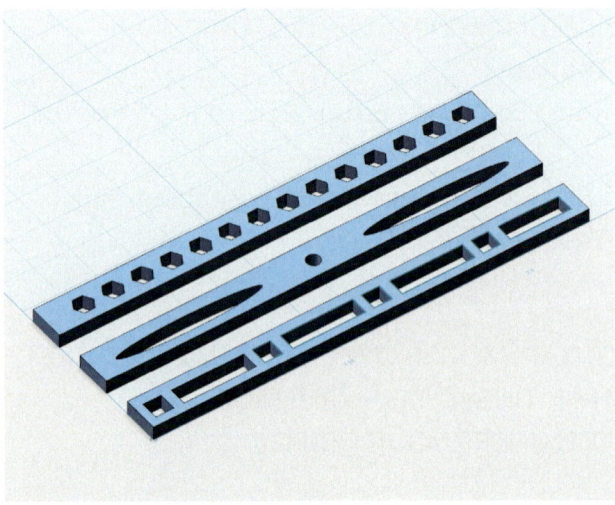

STEP 4: MODIFY MORE TEST BEAMS.

Repeat the process of sketching and extruding to remove more squares and rectangles from your test beam. Some possible test beam designs are shown below. Be creative! What types of beams do you think might be the weakest? The strongest? Why?

- Use what you know to make more test beams, starting again from the same design and dimensions as **Test Beam 1**. Experiment with different buttons and tools to remove different types of holes.

- For example, you might choose the **Circle**, **Ellipse**, or **Polygon** sketches from the **Sketch** menu. How do those tools work?
- If a sketch doesn't turn out the way you like, use Undo and try again. After making a sketch on the beam, extrude it backward through the beam to make it a hole.
- Export and save each beam as an **STL** file, naming them **Test Beam 2**, **Test Beam 3**, and so on.

TIP: YOU CAN EXPORT A PART OF A MODEL IN 123D DESIGN BY SELECTING IT AND THEN CHOOSING **EXPORT SELECTION** FROM THE BOTTOM MENU.

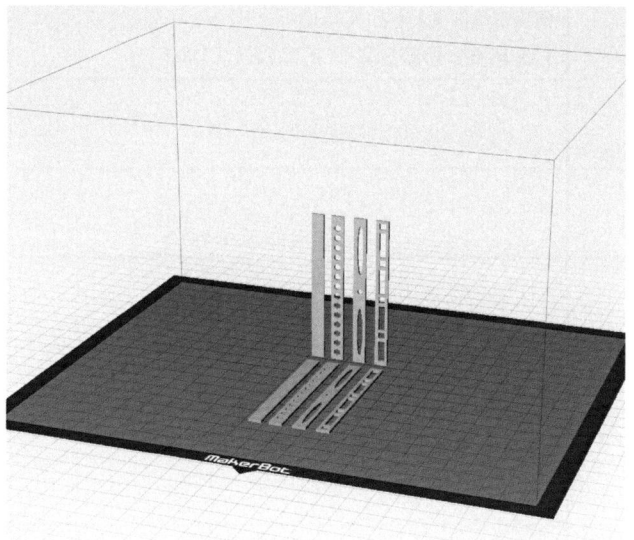

STEP 5: PRINT IN TWO ORIENTATIONS.
- Load the STL files of your test beams into MakerBot Desktop and make sure that they're flat on the build plate.
- Use **copy** and **paste** (or **Duplicate** in the **Edit** menu) to duplicate each beam that you imported. Then reorient all of the copied beams so they're standing vertically, by selecting them and then using **Rotate**.
- Double-check that none of the objects on your build plate are overlapping, and use **Move** to make sure that all of them are touching the build plate.

TIP: EXPERIMENT WITH **EDIT > AUTO LAYOUT** TO QUICKLY ARRANGE YOUR OBJECTS.

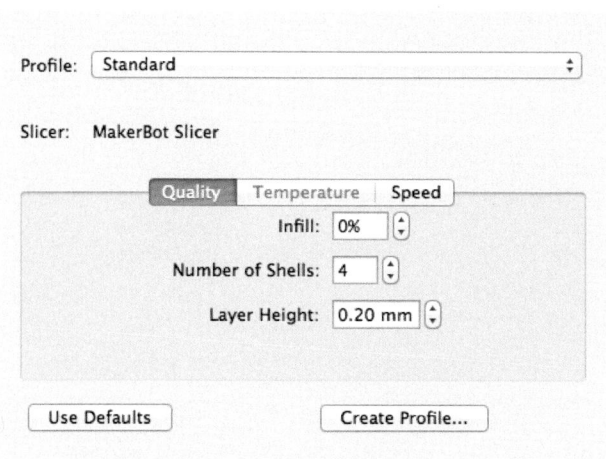

- In **Settings**, set the print job to **Standard** setting with **Raft** but no supports. Then set **Infill** to **0%**, and **Number of Shells** to **4**, and press **Save Settings** (these settings were chosen to result in solid beams). Now print your test beams!

STEP 6: PERFORM A STRESS TEST ON EACH TEST BEAM.

After your test beams are printed, put on safety goggles and test their strength by attempting to break each one. You will notice that certain beams break easier than others. After each beam is broken, look closely at the point at which they broke, the **Break Line**. Observe the similarities and differences of the Break Lines on each beam. Record all findings in a chart like the one shown below. What do these findings mean? You'll be designing bridges using 3D printed components. Based on your observations from this Activity, what should you keep in mind when modeling and printing bridge components to ensure that your bridge can withstand a certain amount of stress without breaking? Experiment with other print settings and orientations and record your findings.

	DIFFICULTY TO BREAK EASY — HARD	**BREAK LINE (WHAT DOES IT LOOK LIKE?)**
Test Beam 1 Horizontal		
Test Beam 1 Vertical		
Test Beam 2 Horizontal		
Test Beam 2 Vertical		
Test Beam 3 Horizontal		
Test Beam 3 Vertical		

CREATE: DESIGN A FOUR-POINT CONNECTOR

When building a large project, it's typical to assemble the structure from a variety of different materials. Using the power of 3D printing, we can create custom connectors to experiment with new and interesting bridge designs. Balsa wood will provide the main structure, and 3D printed components will allow for unique customization. By the end of this section, you'll have created and printed a simple four-point bridge connector, which you can later modify to fit your design criteria.

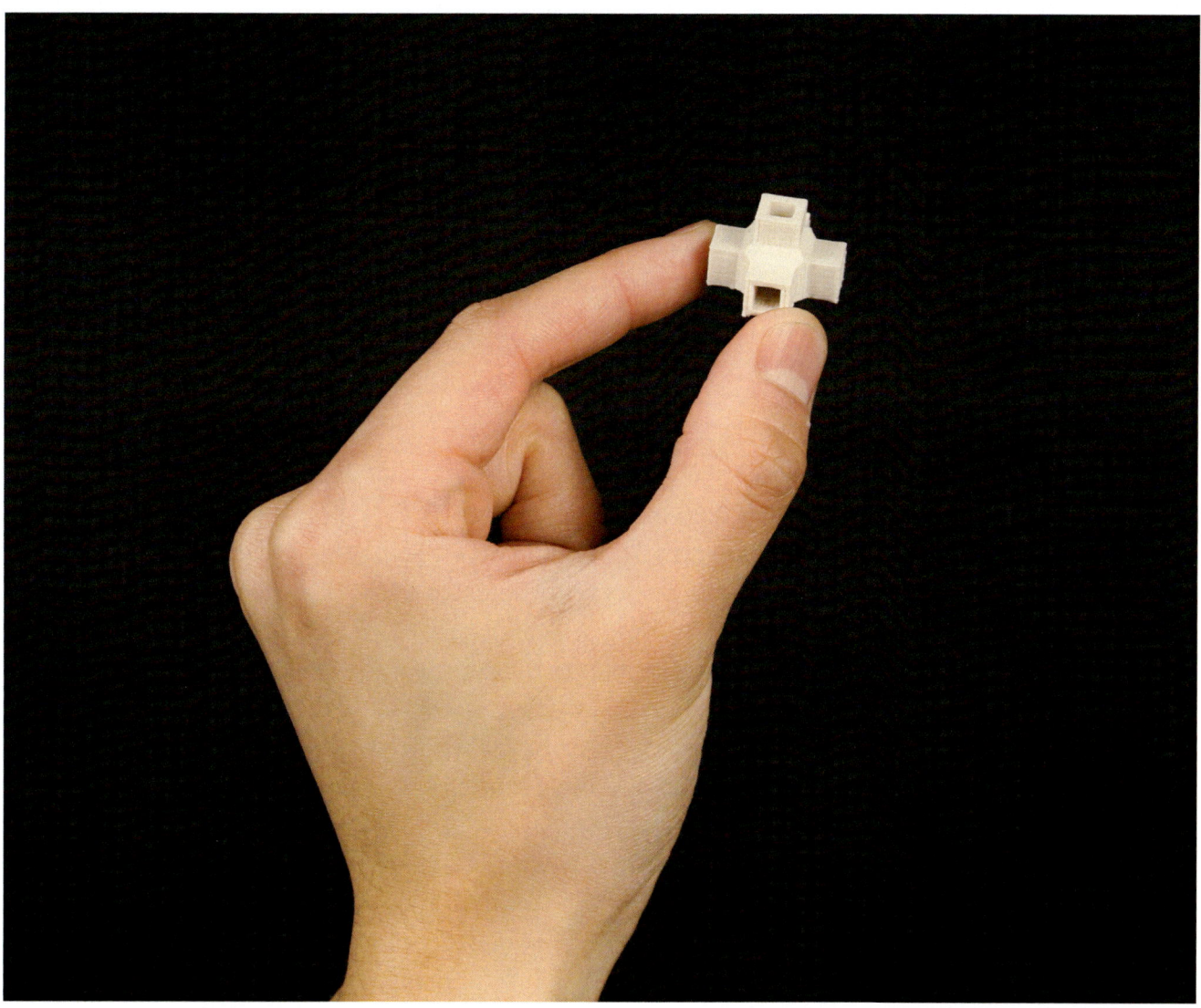

STEP 1: MEASURE YOUR BRIDGE COMPONENTS.
- Use a ruler or calipers to measure the cross section of your balsa wood pieces.

TIP: YOU MAY NEED TO **ORBIT** YOUR VIEW.

- In this project, we're using balsa wood with a square cross section of 1/8 in on each side. Be sure to adjust your design accordingly if you're using differently sized balsa wood.

TIP: RECORD THE VALUE. THIS INFORMATION WILL HELP YOU DESIGN CONNECTORS THAT FIT AROUND THE BALSA WOOD COMPONENTS.

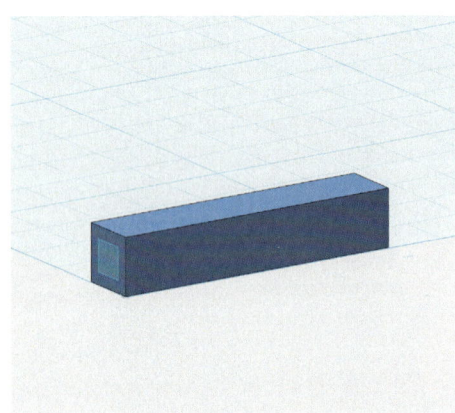

STEP 2: USE PRIMITIVES TO BUILD YOUR CONNECTOR.
In the Explore activity above, you used **Sketch > Rectangle** and **Extrude** to make rectangular holes in an object. In this step, we're going to use a slightly different sketching method. In 123D Design, there's often more than one way to accomplish a task; each way has its own benefits, and you may find that you prefer some more than others.

- In the **Primitives** menu, choose **Box**.
  - Set the dimensions to **0.25 x 1.25 x 0.25 in**.
- In the **Primitives** menu, choose **Rectangle**.
  - Without clicking on anything, move your cursor to the left side of the block you created in the previous step.
  - You should see the center of your rectangle snap to the center of the left side. Don't click anything yet.
  - Leaving your cursor centered on the left face of the block, type in the values **0.14** and **0.14**, and press **Enter/Return** to accept. You should now have a small square centered perfectly on the left face of your block.
    - **Discuss**: Why are these values set to **0.14 in** instead of **0.125 in**?

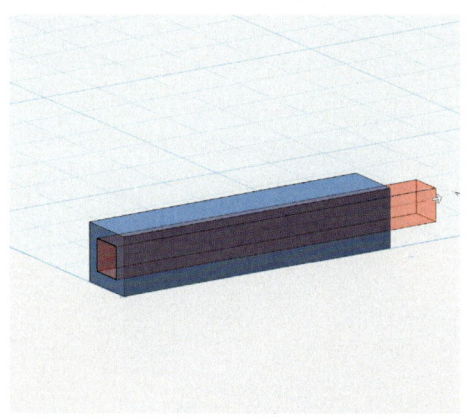

STEP 3: EXTRUDE INTO THE BLOCK TO CREATE A HOLE.
- **Extrude** the square sketch inward through the block. You should now have a hole going all the way through your model to the other side.
- When you're done constructing your model, select **Hide Sketches**.

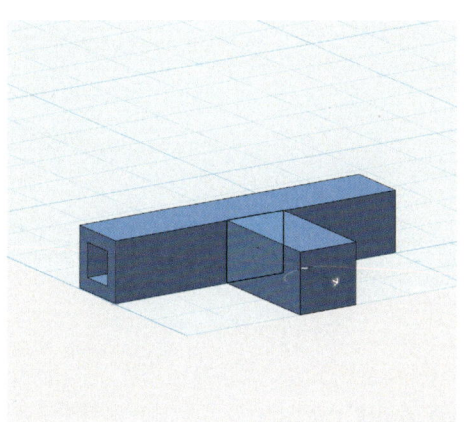

STEP 4: ADD A THIRD CONNECTION POINT.
- Click **Front** on the **View Cube**.
- Use **Sketch > Rectangle** to sketch a **0.25 x 0.25 in** square in the center of the front face of the block.
  Note: Click on the corner of the block to begin sketching.
- Extrude forward to a distance of **0.5 in**.
- Use the same process as **Step 3** to cut a square hole of size **0.14 x 0.14 in** from the center of the new extruded piece.
  Note: This time, the hole should not go all the way through the model.

TIP: YOU MAY NEED TO **ORBIT** TO BE ABLE TO SEE THE EXTRUDE HANDLE.

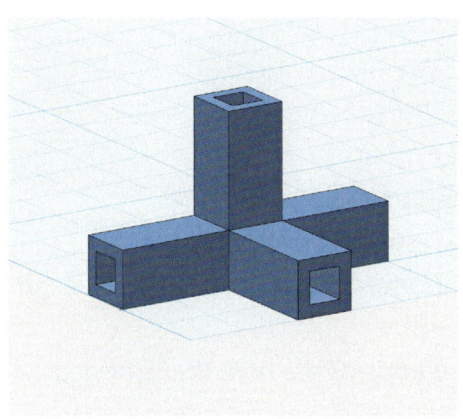

STEP 5: ADD A FOURTH CONNECTION POINT.
- Repeat the process from **Step 4** to create a fourth connection point on the top of your object.

TIP: CLICK **TOP** ON THE **VIEW CUBE**.

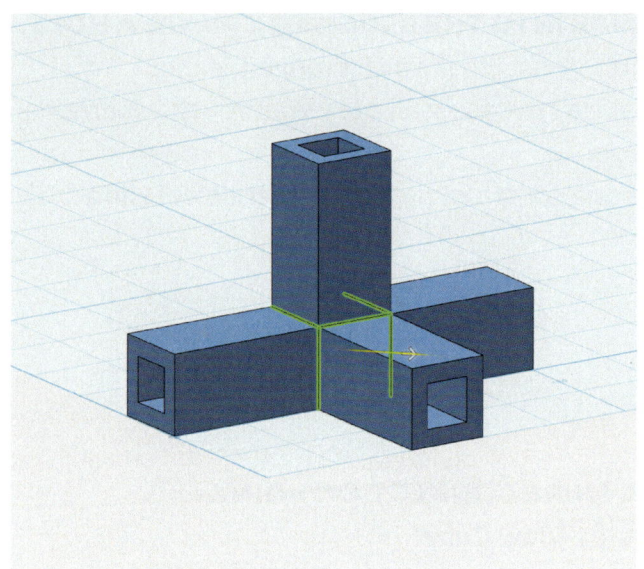 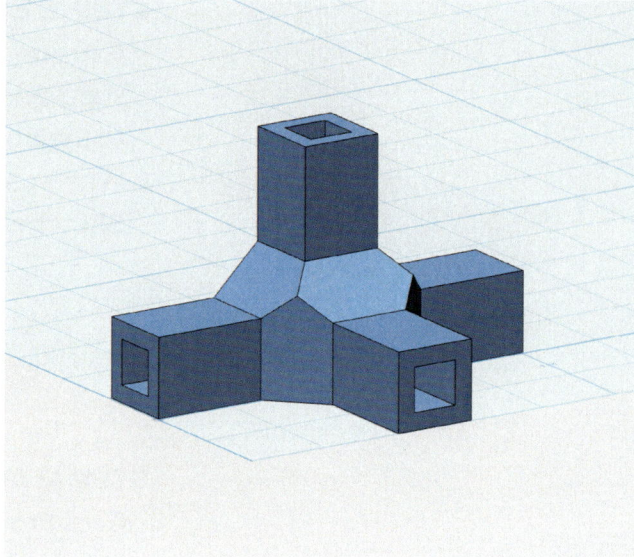

STEP 6: ADD STRENGTH USING THE CHAMFER TOOL.

There are a few weak points in the current design, specifically where the front and top connectors protrude from the original model. You can strengthen these points by adding material with the **Chamfer** tool.

- Select **Modify > Chamfer**.
- One at a time, click to select the five inside-corner edges as shown in the picture.
- Type **0.15** into the value box at the bottom of the screen and press **Enter/Return** to accept. This will create five chamfered edges along the inside weak points of your model. Can you see why this model would be significantly stronger after **chamfering** those edges?

TIP: YOU MAY NEED TO **ORBIT** WHILE SELECTING TO BE
ABLE TO VIEW ALL FIVE OF THE EDGES.

STEP 7: SAVE, EXPORT, AND TEST YOUR FOUR-POINT CONNECTOR.

- Save your work, export the file, import into MakerBot Desktop, and print a test for sizing.
- If your connector is too tight or too loose for your balsa wood components, then adjust your design and print again.

Note: Because of the way that your piece will be 3D printed, the clearance of the hole that extends upward may be different from the clearance of the other holes. Make sure to test this hole separately, and make any necessary adjustments to your design before printing multiple copies of this connector.

CREATE:
DESIGN A HEXAGONAL CONNECTOR

Below is a hexagonal connector with six connection points for balsa wood components.

Instead of sketching a rectangle on a face of the object and then extruding it, we're going to model a 3D stand-in for the balsa wood itself and then copy it in a pattern to make multiple holes in the object.

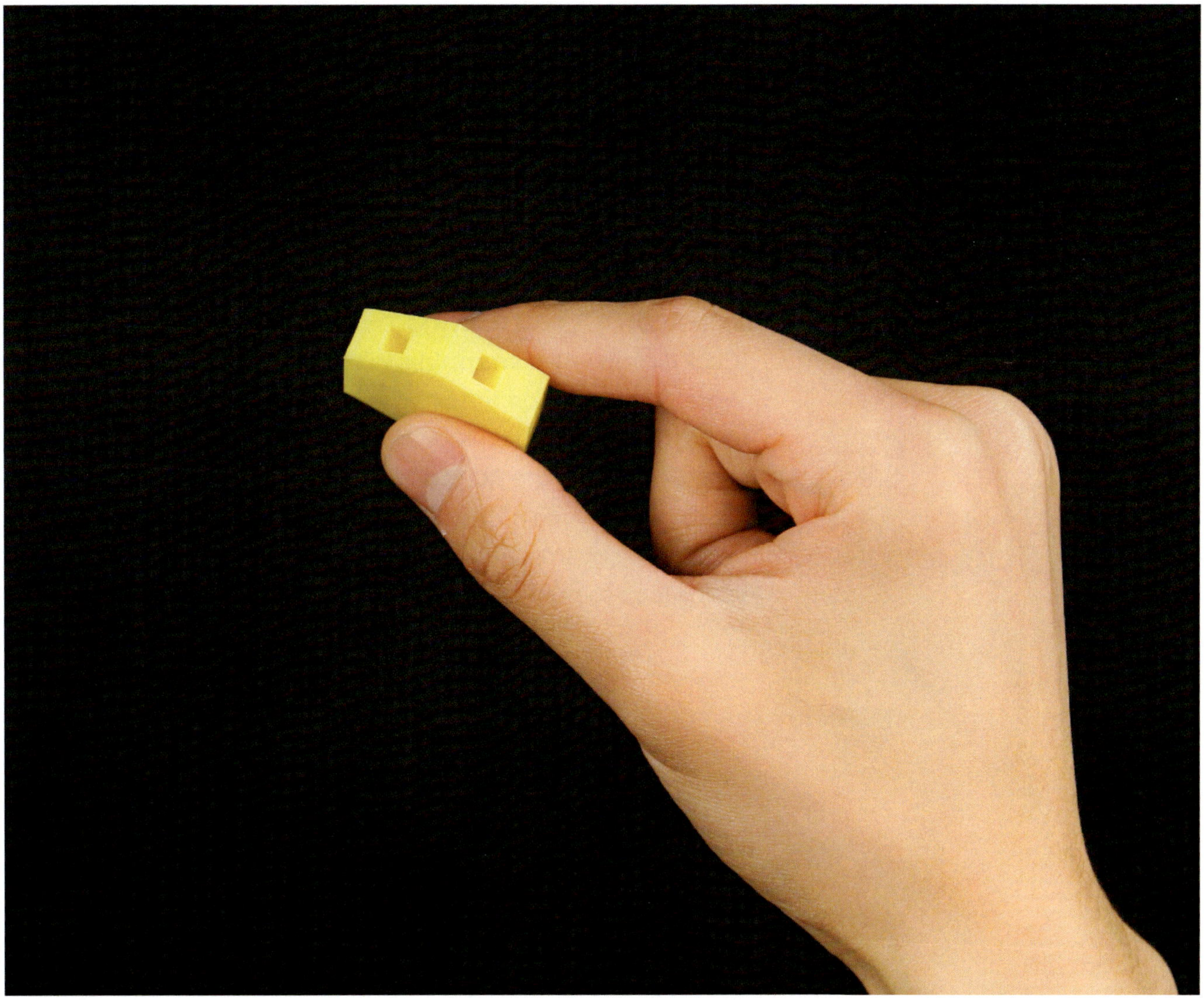

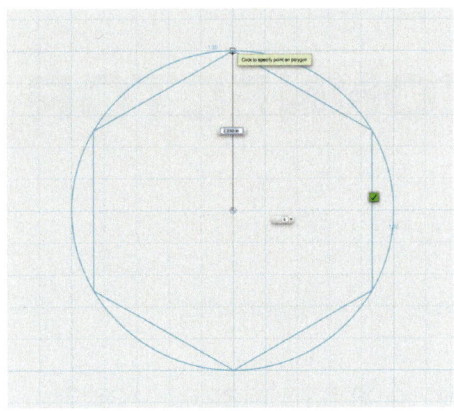

STEP 1: SKETCH AND EXTRUDE A HEXAGONAL PRISM AND A RECTANGULAR BAR.

- Use **Sketch > Polygon** to create a six-sided polygon with radius **1.25 in**.
- **Extrude** forward to a distance of **0.5 in**.

TIPS: CLICK **TOP** ON THE **VIEW CUBE**. YOU MAY NEED TO ORBIT TO BE ABLE TO SEE THE EXTRUDE HANDLE.

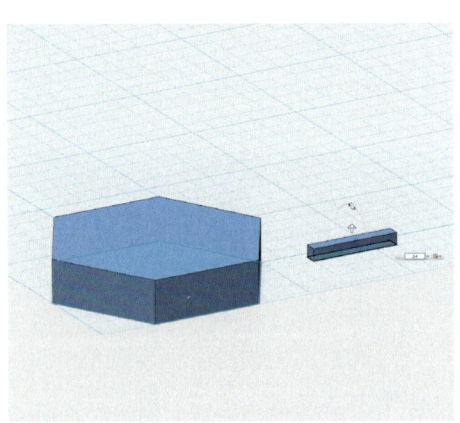

- Use **Sketch > Rectangle** to sketch a **1.0 x 0.14 in** rectangle on the grid next to the hexagonal prism.
- Extrude forward to a distance of **0.14 in**.
  Note: This small block is going to act as a virtual section of balsa wood. We'll use it to subtract out material from the hexagonal prism.
- When you've finished constructing your model, select **Hide Sketches**.

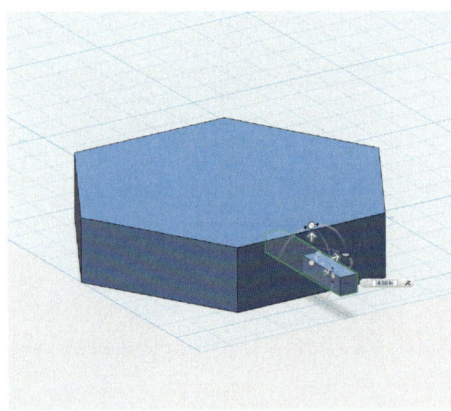

STEP 2: SNAP THE BAR TO THE HEXAGONAL PIECE.

- Click **Group** while **snapping** to turn it off.
  *Note: It's located on the bottom of the **View and Navigation Toolbar**.*
- Use **Snap** from the **3D Modeling Toolbar** to magnetically snap the left face of the rectangle to the front face of the hexagonal prism.
- Use **Move** to push the rectangle into the hexagonal prism.

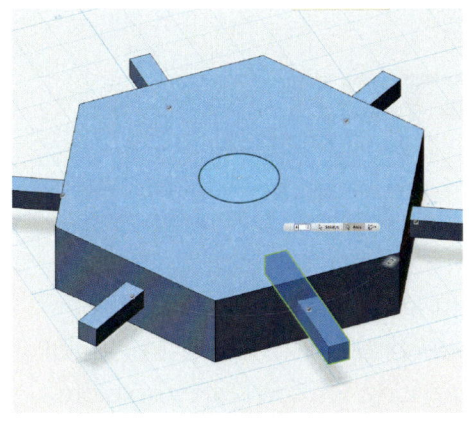

STEP 3: PATTERN THE BAR AROUND ALL SIX SIDES OF THE HEXAGONAL PIECE.

Instead of repeating this process five more times, we can **pattern** the bar around the other five sides of the hexagonal piece.

- Use **Sketch > Circle** to draw a **0.5 in** circle on top of the hexagonal prism.
- Select **Pattern > Circular Pattern** from the **3D Modeling Toolbar**. Select the rectangle as the solid and the circle sketch as the axis. Adjust the number of copies to **6**.

STEP 4: SUBTRACT THE BARS FROM THE HEXAGONAL PIECE TO MAKE HOLES.

- Select **Combine > Subtract** from the **3D Modeling Toolbar**.
- Select the hexagonal prism as the **Target Solid/Mesh**, then click **Source Solid/Mesh** and select each of the six bars.
- **Orbit** around and look at your shape; it should have one square hole in each of the six side faces.

STEP 5: SAVE, EXPORT, AND PRINT.

- Save your 123D Design file and export your design as an **STL** file.
- Load your file into **MakerBot Desktop** and 3D print!

CREATE: DESIGN AN ARC CONNECTOR

We'll now take advantage of the strengths of 3D modeling and printing to explore some unique shapes to consider integrating into your bridge designs. The bulk of your bridge will be constructed of balsa wood, and all of those parts will be straight sections. With 3D printing, we can start to explore shapes that will add personality to your bridge. The examples shown below are just to give you some inspiration. Get creative! You've studied what makes a bridge structure successful, so always keep in mind what impact your design will have on the structural integrity of your bridge.

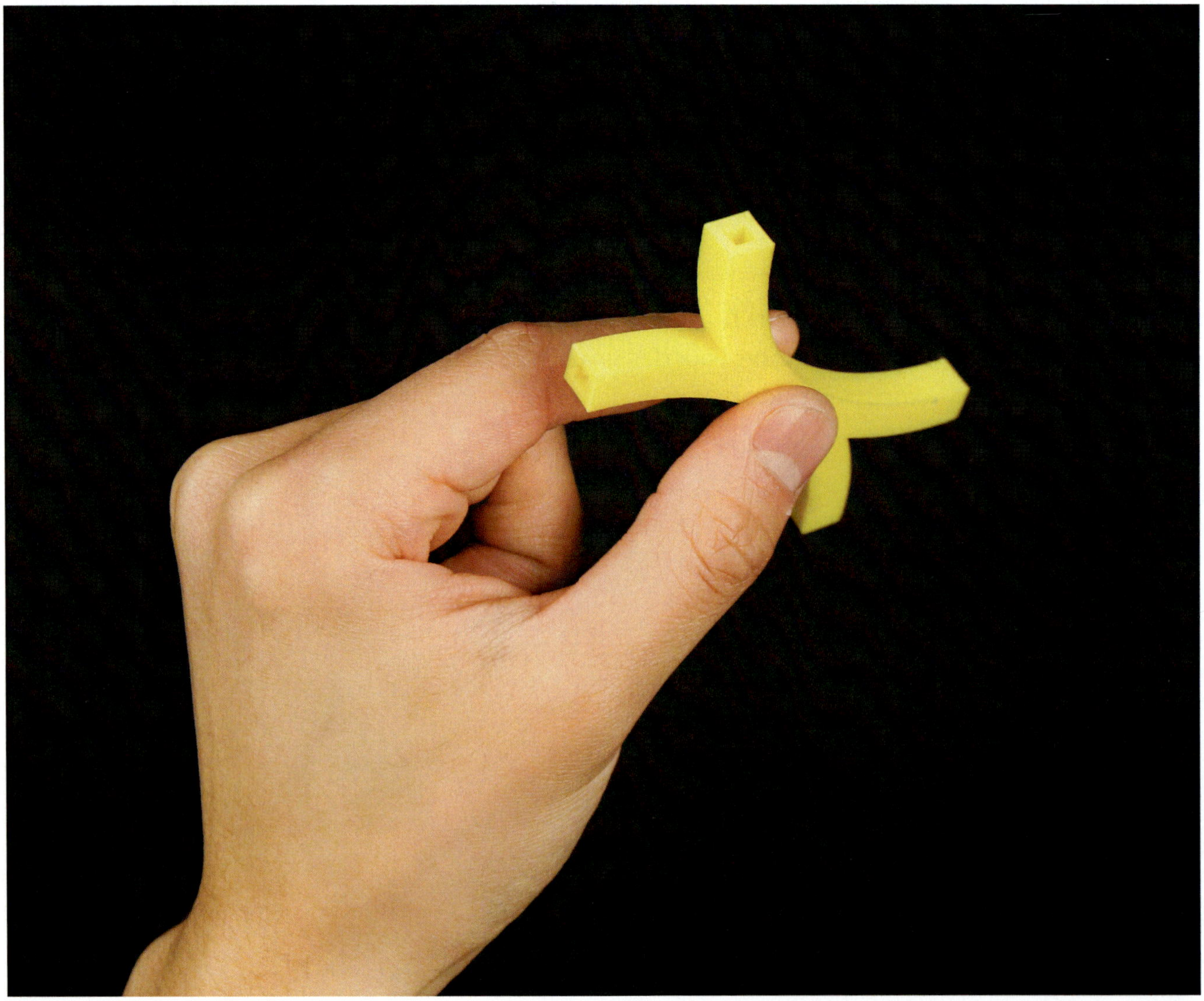

In this lesson, we'll use the **Three Point Arc** tool and the **Offset** tool as we construct this arc-shaped connector piece.

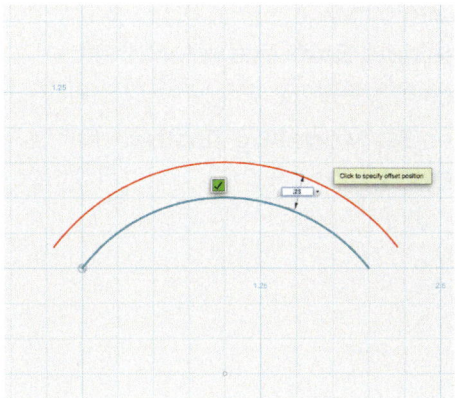

STEP 1: SKETCH AND EXTRUDE AN ARC-SHAPED OBJECT.
- Use **Sketch > Three Point Arc** from the **3D Modeling Tool bar** to draw a **2 x 0.5 in** arc.
- Select **Sketch > Offset** from the **3D Modeling Toolbar** and click on your three point arc. Move your cursor upward **0.25 in**.
- We want to make this a solid sketch. Use **Sketch > Polyline** to connect the arcs.
- Use **Construct > Extrude** to extrude this arc shape upward to **0.25 in**.

TIP: CLICK ON THE **WORKPLANE** TO START SKETCHING, THEN CLICK ON THE ORIGIN TO SET THE FIRST POINT, AND CLICK **2** IN TO THE LEFT TO SET THE SECOND. FINALLY, MOVE THE CURSOR UPWARD UNTIL THE ARC HAS A HEIGHT OF **0.5 IN**. THE SKETCH WILL FILL IN WITH A BLUE SHADE WHEN COMPLETE.

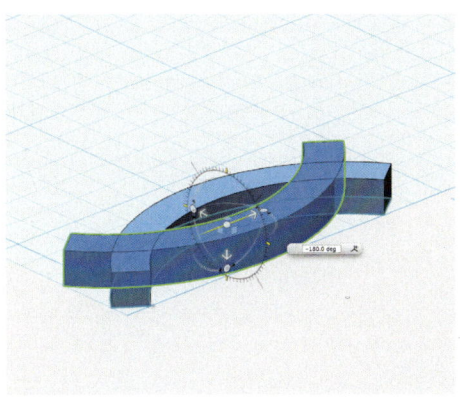

STEP 2: CREATE AND MERGE A DOUBLE-ARC SHAPE.
- **Copy/Paste** your arc to create another and use **Transform** to rotate the new one **180°** and move it back **0.5 in**.
  Note: The result should be an arc "X" shape, like the image on the left.
- Use **Combine > Merge** from the **3D Modeling Toolbar** to combine the two arcs into one single piece.
  - Choose one arc object as the **Target Arc/Mesh**, then press **Source Solid/Mesh** to merge.

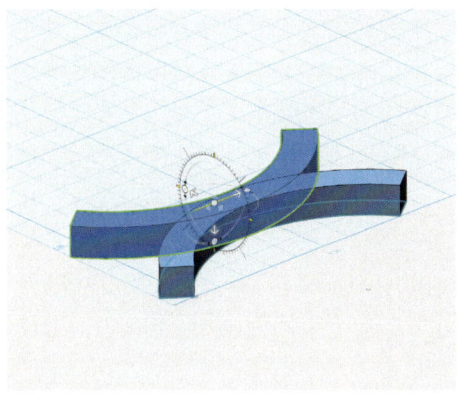

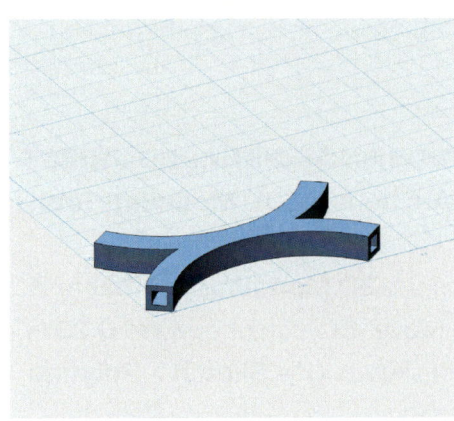

STEP 3: HOLLOW OUT THE FOUR ENDS OF THE DOUBLE-ARC SHAPE.

We can't use our previous methods to hollow out the ends of this shape, because the ends are curvy.

- Click on your object and then hold **Shift** and select the four faces on the end of each arc.
- Use **Modify > Shell** from the **3D Modeling Toolbar** to hollow out the object to **0.055 in**.

TIP: YOU CAN USE THE **PILL ICON** THAT APPEARS NEXT TO YOUR CURSOR TO QUICKLY ACCESS THE SHELL OPTION.

Note: We used the value **0.055 in** because it's half of the difference between **0.25 in** and **0.14 in**. If you used a value other than **0.14 in** based on your sizing tests, then use a correspondingly different value than **0.055 in**.

CREATE: DESIGN ADDITIONAL CONNECTORS

The picture shows a few more types of connectors for inspiration. How do you think these were made?

Imagine new types of connectors that will help you design your bridge, and use your 123D Design knowledge to achieve them. Experiment with 123D Design tools and see what other kinds of connectors you can make. Remember to print sample parts to test-fit your balsa wood before printing large quantities of connectors.

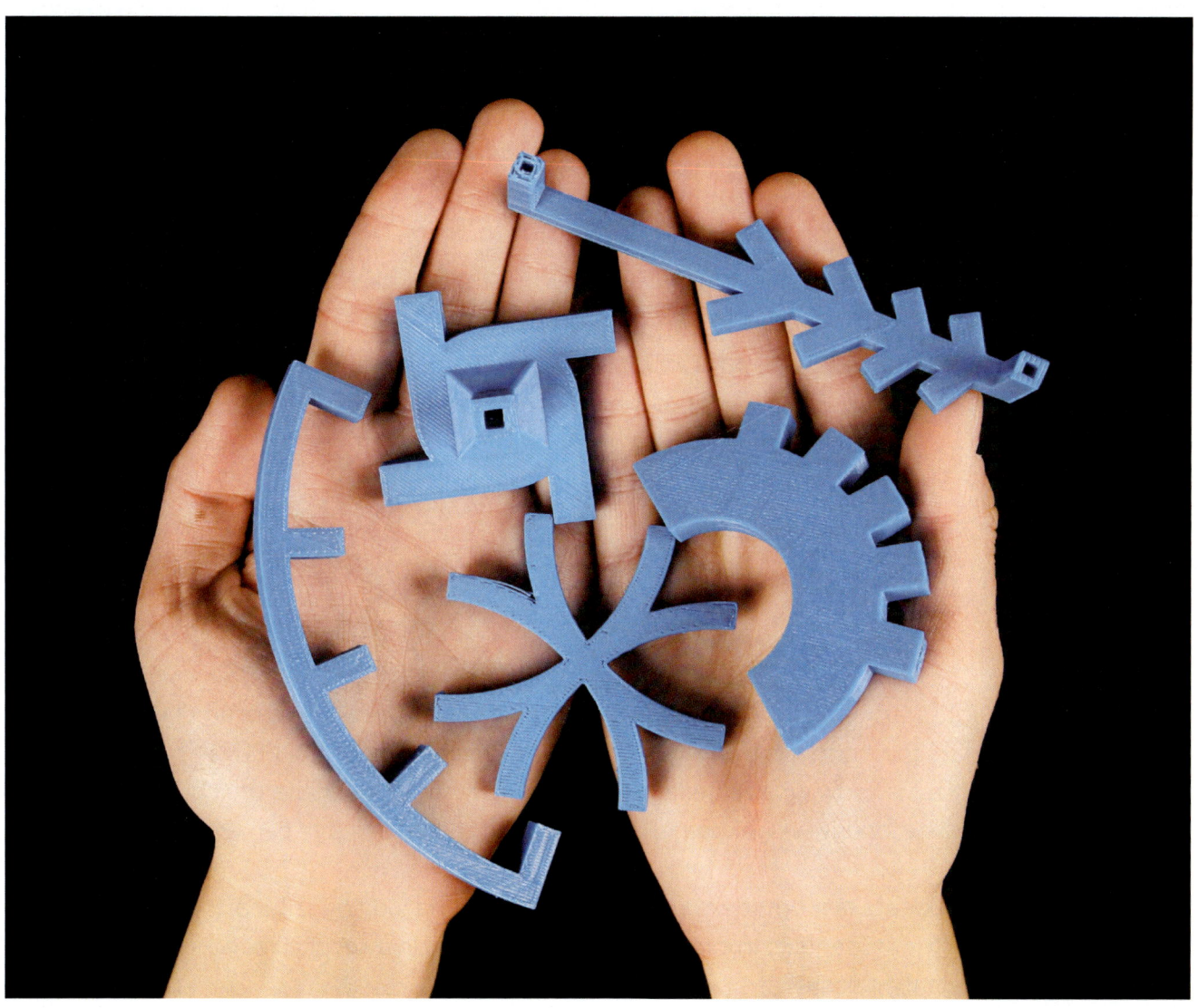

FURTHER ACTIVITIES: BRIDGE TESTING, UPCYCLED STRUCTURES

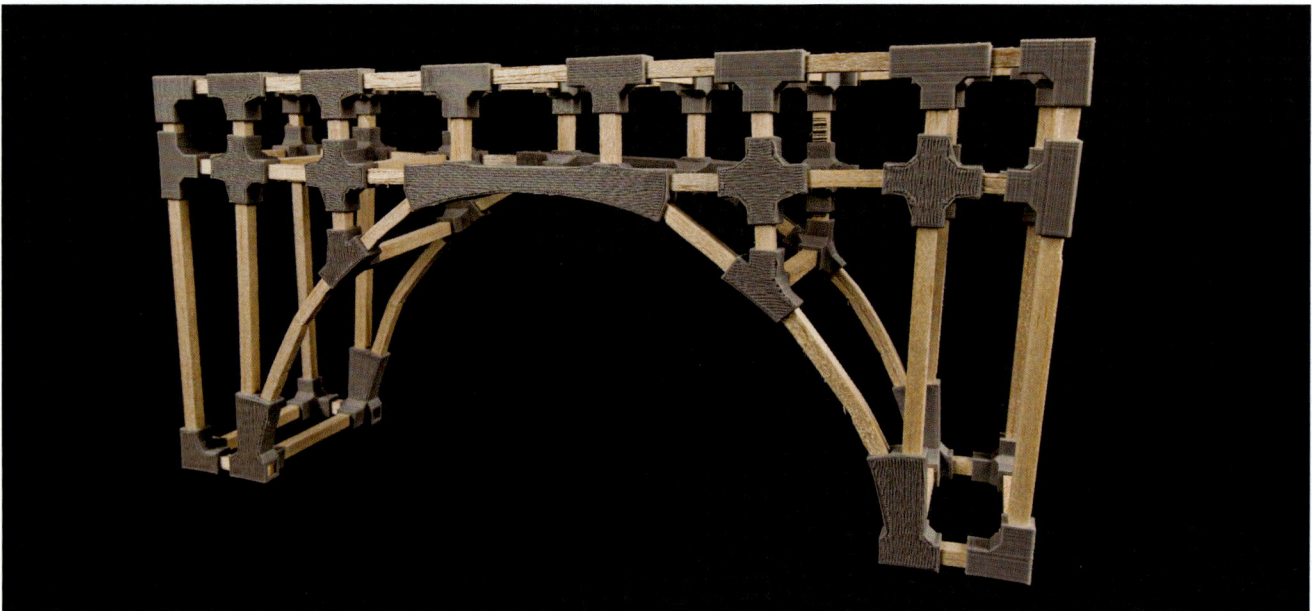

ACTIVITY 1: DESIGN, BUILD, AND TEST A BRIDGE.
Students can work in teams to design and build bridges using their 3D printed connector pieces.

Materials
- Balsa wood dowels
- Wood glue
- 3D printed connector pieces

Steps
1. Have your students start by sketching out their ideas on graph paper. They can label their sketches to indicate the materials they plan to use for each element of the bridge.
2. Make sure the students know what criteria will be used to test and evaluate their bridge designs. Some options are size, bridge weight, material use, weight that the bridge can withstand, and aesthetics.
3. Finally, have the students test out their bridges according to the judging criteria.
4. If there's time, ask the students to improve their bridge designs in a second round, to see if they can raise their evaluation scores.

5. Enthusiasts can take things further by exploring print-in-place hinges and mechanisms to create a drawbridge, or by creating extra 3D printed parts to reinforce or decorate their bridges.

ACTIVITY 2: CREATE UPCYCLED STRUCTURES WITH 3D PRINTED CONNECTORS.

Use 3D printed connectors to create new structures out of recycled or found materials.

Materials
- Recycled or found materials for main structure pieces
- 3D printed connector pieces

Steps
1. Find materials for building, such as dowels, leftover art supplies, paper towel rolls, and items from the recycling bin — whatever you have on hand. Try to find objects that you have a lot of, or that have similar types of ends or areas for connecting.
2. Have the students brainstorm about what they can make with the found materials. An Eiffel Tower? A skyscraper? A spaceship? Different building materials will be suitable for different types of structures, so think about what each material could best be used to build.
3. Have the students use 123D Design to build connectors for attaching and assembling the objects into new structures. What kinds of connectors are needed for the types of objects that you found?

KNOWLEDGE CHECKS
- What are the different types of bridge structures? What are their strengths and weaknesses?
- How does the shape of a bridge determine the amount of force it can withstand? What geometric shapes are commonly used in bridge design?
- How do print orientation and settings affect the strength of your printed parts?
- What considerations are important when designing parts that fit together?
- What are two different ways to create a 3D object in 123D Design?

MOVING FORWARD
Solid modeling tools like 123D Design are useful for making functional parts and complex assemblies. As you experienced in the bridge building project, making small parts with specific dimensions allows you to create large complex structures. Engineers, architects, and many other professionals use similar software programs to create extremely complex structures like cars and buildings. As you progress in your solid modeling skills, know that the foundation 123D Design gives you will translate easily into more advanced software.

ADVANCED 3D PRINTING TECHNIQUES AND TROUBLESHOOTING

USING AUTODESK MESHMIXER IN 3D PRINTING

As you continue to experiment with printing models, you will start to notice aspects of files that result in them printing better or worse than others. Some files even have issues that prevent them from printing successfully no matter how many settings you alter. In such cases, you'll have to experiment with fixing the file so its prints reliably. In this section, we'll look at common issues, how to find them and ways to fix them. Then we'll examine a few ways to use MeshMixer as a print utility.

LEARNING OBJECTIVES
- Be able to recognize broken files
- Identify what is causing an issue
- Analyze and repair broken files
- Explore advanced printing techniques using MeshMixer

TERMINOLOGY
- **Non-manifold:** A mesh that's not complete or sealed, with polygons missing or intersecting
- **Watertight:** A continuous outside surface (or **mesh**), necessary for successful 3D printing. For example, an object like a donut, even though it has a hole in the middle, has a continuous outside surface and could be 3D printed.
- **Reverse normals:** When a polygon's direction is opposite from that of the rest of the model's polygons
- **Triangles:** Synonymous with "polygons"
- **Vertices:** The points where polygons/triangles meet

RECOGNIZING BROKEN FILES
- **What is a broken model?** A broken model is a file that you won't be able to print, no matter what settings you choose in **MakerBot Desktop**.
- **What does it look like?** The best way to discover a broken model is to use **MakerBot Desktop's Print Preview**.
  - When viewing a file in **Print Preview**, scroll through the layers and make sure that the **infill** pattern and the **support structures** are where they should be.
  - **It's highly recommended that you always check Print Preview before printing.**

Note: Infill is inside your model and supports are outside. If infill or supports are in the wrong place, or any extra material is where it shouldn't be, your file may be broken.

WHAT EXACTLY IS WRONG WITH MY MODEL?
Below are a few examples that outline the most common issues.

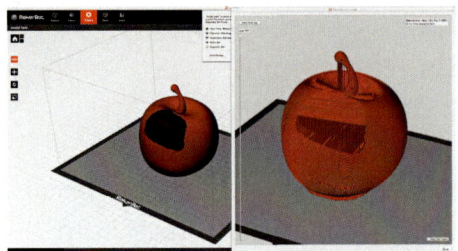

There are holes in my model:
If you notice a section of your model is missing or an area appears darkened in **Print Preview**, you likely have an issue with your **mesh**.

- **Non-manifold:** MakerBot Desktop cannot determine the boundaries of your print because the mesh that makes up your model is incomplete. This can happen in 3D modeling programs when **polygons** are missing from the surface of your model. **Manifold** is also referred to as **Watertight**.
- **Reverse normals:** MakerBot Desktop cannot differentiate the inside of the model from the outside. One or more **polygons** of your model's **mesh** are flipped inside out. Every polygon has a direction, and its direction points either inward or outward. For a model to print, all polygons need to point in the same direction. A file with **reverse normals** is also considered **non-manifold**.

Part of my model is missing:
If you notice that pieces of your model are missing when you import the file into **MakerBot Desktop**, they were not properly combined before export from your design program. You may see the following:

- Part of your model fails to appear upon import into **MakerBot Desktop**.
- In **Print Preview**, parts of your object appear as though they're building independent of each other, when they should be treated as a single object.

HOW DO I FIX IT?
If possible, we find the best way to fix a model is to open the file in the program in which it was originally designed and attempt to repair the issue.

If the original design file is not available, take the **STL** or **OBJ** file and import it into a repair program like Autodesk MeshMixer. MeshMixer is a troubleshooting program that has a lot of analysis and repair tools. Similar programs, such as Netfabb and MeshLab, are also available.

USING MESHMIXER

Autodesk MeshMixer is a free downloadable software program. It's one of the most powerful free troubleshooting and print utility programs currently available. You can use it to design and manipulate models as well, but its most powerful function is optimizing files for 3D printing.

MeshMixer navigation and tips:
- When in MeshMixer, import the apple.
- In the **Menu** bar, click **MeshMixer > Preferences > File**. At the very top of this dialogue box is a checkbox labeled **Flip Z-Y axis on Import-Export**. Click this checkbox. This will help when you export your model from MeshMixer into MakerBot Desktop. Your axes will be the same in both programs.
- Navigation: In **Preferences > General > Navigation Mode > 123D Apps** (Default)
  Orbit: Drag right mouse
  Pan: Drag mouse wheel button
  Zoom: Scroll mouse wheel
- A three-button mouse is preferable for using MeshMixer. Navigation without a three-button mouse means you'll need to use the spacebar to select the navigation tools.

REPAIRING FILES

The easiest and most effective repair tool in MeshMixer is in the print utility.

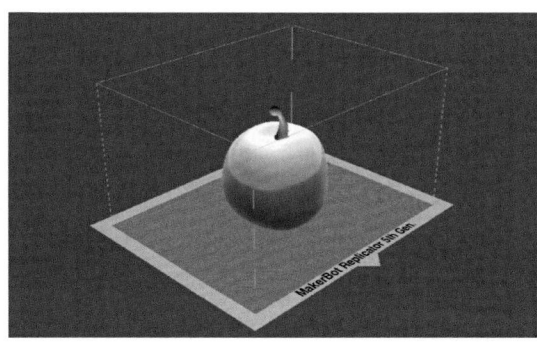

- Import your broken model and click the **Print** button on the left menu.
- Click **Repair Selected**. The repair could take from a few seconds to several minutes.
- When it's completed, look around the model to make sure the file has been fixed.
- Export your repaired model and import it to **MakerBot Desktop**.

USING MESHMIXER FOR ADVANCED PRINTING TECHNIQUES

CUSTOM SUPPORTS

When you prepare your model in **MakerBot Desktop**, is your print encased in supports? If so, it might be a good time to try out MeshMixer's support generator. MeshMixer provides more control over how the support structures are generated. To generate custom supports, follow these steps.
- Import your model and click the **Print** button to enter the print utility.
- Scale your model to the desired print size in the **Transform** menu.
- Click **Add Supports** to generate support material under all overhangs.
  - Select the **tool icon** to customize your support structures.

- Hold **Shift** and **click+drag** to add additional supports as desired.
- **Ctrl/Cmd+click** to delete existing supports.
- Export the **STL** and import it into MakerBot Desktop.
  - Be sure that supports are not selected in the settings in MakerBot Desktop before printing.

SEPARATING PRINT FILES

Sometimes you may want to access the parts of an **STL** or **OBJ** file separately. The **Separate Shells** tool will allow you to break out each individual piece. Here are some reasons why you would do that:

- Printing parts of a file in different colors
- Organizing the parts on your build plate differently
- Changing print settings for different pieces (e.g., one part with higher infill, other parts with lower)
- Some parts are floating in the air and need to be moved down to the build plate
- Dual extrusion printing

To separate a file into multiple objects, follow the steps below:
- Click on the **Separate Shells** tool, located in the **Edit** menu on the left side of your screen. In the **Object Browser**, you'll now have two or more objects.
- Export each object one at a time.

PRINTING LARGER MODELS IN PIECES

Sometimes you may want to print an object that's larger than your build plate. There are several ways to accomplish this, but one of the easiest is to use the **Make Slices** tool. This allows you to slice an object into many pieces and print each individually. You can then assemble them to make a large model.

To use the **Make Slices** tool, follow these steps:
- Import the model at your desired scale.
- Select **Edit > Make Slices**, and change **Method** to **Stacked3D**.
- Pick your axis and select the thickness you want for each piece.
- Click **Compute** to preview the slices.
- Click **Accept**. All the slices will appear as separate objects in the **Object Browser**.
- Export each one as an **STL** or **OBJ** for printing.

REDUCING THE NUMBER OF POLYGONS/TRIANGLES IN A 3D MESH

When preparing certain models in **MakerBot Desktop**, you may notice that slicing times are unusually long. This is likely because your model has a very high polygon count (similar to a high-resolution picture). In MeshMixer, you can reduce the number of polygons to speed up your **MakerBot Desktop** slicing process.

To reduce the number of polygons in your model, follow the steps below:

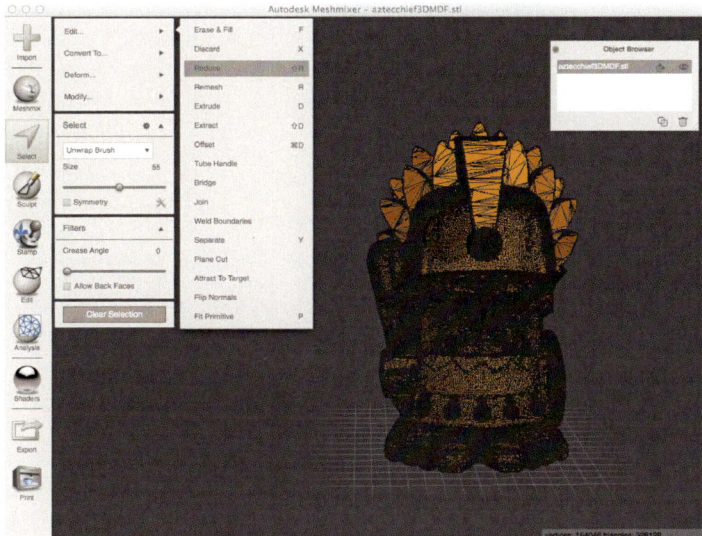

- Import your model into MeshMixer.
- Check the vertex and triangle counts in the bottom right corner. The triangle count should be below 100,000.
- Check the wireframe view with the hotkey **W** to get a visual of the triangle count.
- To reduce the polygon count, select the entire model using **cmd/ctrl + a**.
- Select **Edit > Reduce**, type in a percentage, and press Enter to accept.
- Adjust the percentage higher or lower as needed until your triangle count is close to or under 100,000.

Note: Reducing the polygon count too far will mean loss of detail in your model.
- When you're done updating the file, click **Accept**, and export your model for printing.

KNOWLEDGE CHECKS
- What is a non-manifold model?
- How can you find out if your model is broken?
- What are some of the advanced printing techniques you can do in MeshMixer?

WHAT'S NEXT
When designing a model from scratch, there are important considerations for ensuring that it will 3D print successfully. If the model was not designed with these considerations in mind, issues can arise when trying to 3D print it. It's best to fix those issues in the original modeling program, but if that's not possible, repair programs like MeshMixer, Netfabb, or MeshLab can be immensely useful.

CONCLUSION AND NEXT STEPS

KNOWLEDGE CHECKS
Teachers
- How 3D printers work, on both a hardware and software level
- How to set up and maintain a 3D printer
- How to integrate 3D printing into a range of class topics
- Understand the variety of 3D modeling software and when to use certain types
- Create objects in the 3D modeling software programs outlined in the projects

Students
- How 3D printers work, on both a hardware and software level
- Work with their peers to create 3D prints
- Understand the importance of iterations in design
- Real-world applications of 3D printing and design

MAKE YOUR OWN 3D PRINTING CONTRIBUTION TO THE CLASSROOM

It's time to begin brainstorming your next 3D printing project. Think about the projects you need to cover this year in the classroom. Think about which of these topics include a project that involves your students creating something physical. Even if these projects are creating a book, drawing pictures, playing with clay, making a plane, or reporting on a president, you can incorporate MakerBot. The only boundary is your imagination.

As you come up with ideas for 3D printing projects, share them with the community on Thingiverse!

Some ideas you might want to explore further are:
History: Make a diorama of a historical landmark or city. Prompt students to model and print a component of the diorama and share what printed parts they chose to incorporate.
Math: If you're exploring fractals, consider having your students design and demonstrate these ideas with 3D printed visuals.
Science: Consider printing out snap together DNA molecules to demonstrate how DNA is built. Have students design plant and animal cell models as a class project.
English: 3D model and print a companion object for a book report. Students can design an important object or scene and describe how they decided on its appearance.
Art: 3D model and print different clay tools such as a patterned edge coat modeling tool, a stamp, or a mold form.
Drama & Theater: Collaboratively 3D model, print, and assemble a prop that will appear in a play.

USING THIS BOOK AS YOUR LAUNCHPAD

By now we hope you agree that 3D printing and modeling provide a rich and engaging way to enhance the skills being taught in your classroom. No matter what the subject, your journey through 3D printing will present you and your students with real-world challenges and opportunities to incorporate hands-on problem solving into your curriculum.

Throughout this book we have highlighted many different approaches to 3D printing in the classroom. The start of any project begins with finding inspiration. Once you feel confident printing a variety of different kinds of 3D models, push yourself to design more and more complex ones. Try reverse engineering something you interact with everyday. Review the projects you already use in your classes and look for ways that 3D printing can enhance these experiences for you and your students.

Teaching your students about 3D printing doesn't end at the completion of this book. Use your 3D printers just like any other tool you have around your classroom. Empower your students to take chances and make mistakes because they are only limited by their imagination. Get out there and start making.

ACKNOWLEDGMENTS

This book was the brainchild and creative endeavor of a small army of 3D printing and design enthusiasts and gurus. Thanks for the inspiring teamwork to bring *MakerBot in the Classroom* to life.

Content
Mike Amundsen
Erin Arden
Drew Lentz
Poppy Lyttle
Laura Taalman

Marketing
Colby Dennison

Creative
Christopher Salyers
Sonal Chakrasali

Photographer
Stephanie Banares

Special Thanks
Mary Boniece
Brian Kimmelblatt
Eric Mortensen
Leslie Perry
Parker Thomas
Richard Vicenzi

MakerBot Education
Allison Vicenzi

At MakerBot, we are committed to making 3D printing more accessible for everyone. Educators integrating 3D printing and design into their classrooms and lessons are instrumental in this goal of widespread accessibility. As the future of 3D printing continues to be defined, MakerBot Education is determined to work together with educators to provide the tools and resources to empower students to design and create. Thank you for your continued dedication to preparing students for the future. We can't wait to see what you make!